The Management Book

FT Prentice Hall
FINANCIAL TIMES

In an increasingly competitive world, we believe it's quality of
thinking that gives you the edge – an idea that opens new
doors, a technique that solves a problem, or an insight that
simply makes sense of it all. The more you know, the smarter
and faster you can go.

That's why we work with the best minds in business and finance
to bring cutting-edge thinking and best learning practice to a
global market.

Under a range of leading imprints, including *Financial Times
Prentice Hall*, we create world-class print publications and
electronic products bringing our readers knowledge, skills and
understanding which can be applied whether studying or at work.

To find out more about Pearson Education publications, or
tell us about the books you'd like to find, you can visit us at
www.pearson.com/uk

The Management Book

Richard Newton

**Financial Times
Prentice Hall
is an imprint of**

Harlow, England • London • New York • Boston • San Francisco • Toronto
Sydney • Tokyo • Singapore • Hong Kong • Seoul • Taipei • New Delhi
Cape Town • Madrid • Mexico City • Amsterdam • Munich • Paris • Milan

PEARSON EDUCATION LIMITED

Edinburgh Gate
Harlow CM20 2JE
Tel: +44 (0)1279 623623
Fax: +44 (0)1279 431059
Website: www.pearson.com/uk

First published in Great Britain in 2011

© Richard Newton 2011

The right of Richard Newton to be identified as author of this work has been
asserted by him in accordance with the Copyright, Designs and Patents Act 1988.

Pearson Education is not responsible for the content of third-party internet sites.

ISBN: 978–0–273–75033–8

British Library Cataloguing-in-Publication Data
A catalogue record for this book is available from the British Library

Library of Congress Cataloging-in-Publication Data
Newton, Richard, 1964-
  The management book : mastering the art of leading teams / Richard Newton.
    p. cm.
  Includes index.
  ISBN 978-0-273-75033-8 (pbk.)
  1. Teams in the workplace--Management. 2. Management. I. Title
  HD66.N49 2011
  658.4'022--dc23
                              2011027634

10 9 8 7 6 5 4 3
15 14 13 12

Designed by Sue Lamble
Typeset in 9/13pt ITC Stone Serif Std by 3
Printed by Ashford Colour Press Ltd, Gosport

Contents

Acknowledgements

A good teacher is a blessing. Their impact extends beyond their subject and continues after the lesson is finished. This book is dedicated to:

- Hilary Bailey
- Sensei Ian Patterson

Preface

In setting out to write this book I wanted to create something unique, novel and value adding. Not an easy challenge given the numbers of management books in existence. I have avoided the paths many management writers have travelled before and, hopefully, have created an interesting and unusual perspective on management. One that will help managers come to terms with their roles and to find ways to excel.

To provide rapid, accessible advice I have designed an easy-to-follow format and structure: the book is broken into 36 articles, organised into 9 themed parts. The articles cover the range of management issues and concerns. They can be read end-to-end, or you can dip in and read any one article by itself.

I like exposing the assumptions we make about management. There are many unquestioned and often unreasonable assumptions in management thinking. These assumptions limit our performance and achievement of our objectives. By exposing them we can examine them and then accept, improve or reject them.

Management should be at the centre of business thinking. But managers are the often forgotten heroes of business. In business writing and discourse there is a focus on topics like leadership, empowered workers, and the web phenomenon of voluntary collaborative participation. I do not doubt the value of these topics, but there is a tendency in focusing on them to squeeze management out of the picture. Worse than this, managers are blamed for all the past ills of the company. Think of how the phrase 'middle manager' is used almost as a term of abuse in organisations.

Poor management is the cause of many business ills, but every good business has good management. Without managers, empowered workers have insufficient direction and guidance; all leaders are managers too, and collaborative participation has its limits and even it needs some form of management.

We have lost sight of the centrality of management to business, and the centrality of teams to the manager's role. Topics like leadership are important. The thinking on it over the last few decades has been helpful, but it often obscures the fact that leaders do not spring from nowhere. Leadership is crucial, but it is just one part of the manager's role.

The character of management has changed and continues to change. With this comes a need to focus on different skills and competencies. Yet management is and will remain essential to business. The articles in this book will support you in retaining up-to-date skills and remaining an essential component of whatever business you work in.

Introduction

Management is not always seen as an exciting topic. This is odd given how critical it is to business. Successful businesses may thrive on creativity and innovation, but it is good management that makes them effective and efficient. When a business fails, you can be certain the finger will soon point to poor management. Perhaps we do not consider management enough because we take it for granted. We should not. Examples of poor management are everywhere. On top of this, management is changing and will continue to change in response to the evolution of business and society.

But what is management? Irrespective of the situation, a manager manages a team to get something done. If tasks are not complex, large scale or benefiting from labour specialisation there is no need for a team. If there is no team, there is no need for a manager. But many tasks need teams and those teams need managers. That, in essence, is the scope of this book: the manager's role in managing teams to get things done.

There is a large variation in what business teams do, and how they do it. So large that it might be thought impossible to write about management in a general sense. Management is context-specific. Management cannot be learnt by reading books or attending courses – management is learnt by experience.

I approach the topic by helping you decide what is right for you. I assist you to explore and understand your own situation. I expose the decisions managers make and the implications of choosing one way to manage over another.

The contents

The choice of this book's contents follows a deliberate plan. I have tried to stick to the essential parts of management, but to look at them from unusual perspectives and different angles. I have taken the approach of seeking out the underlying assumptions in beliefs and behaviours with regard to management, exposing them and challenging them. My belief is that we don't do this enough in management.

The contents give an honest view of management. I do not take the corporate line. Some aspects of management are not appealing to everyone, but by openly thinking about them you can decide how to face them, and even if management is the right career for you.

The structure

This book has been split into nine parts, each of which focuses on an important management theme. The parts are sub-divided into four sections, each containing one article. The articles are varied, but when combined provide a comprehensive view on the theme of the part. Although the articles build into a picture of management, they are designed to stand alone. You can pick any section in any part of the book and read it as an individual piece of advice.

Each of the articles is short, and can easily be read in one sitting. To ease use, the articles are all structured in the same way.

How to use the book

There are two ways to use this book. I hope you find both of them useful.

Read it end-to-end to gain an overall picture of management. There is a rough logical ordering to the parts, from Part 1 starting with the basics, and progressing to more sophisticated and complex managerial issues. There are cross-references between the articles to help you build a complex, flexible and many-sided view of management.

Alternatively, dip in and pick the articles that are most helpful to you. Each article is complete as a stand-alone read. Use the book as a reference source, reading articles as and when you want. Hopefully, you will come back to the book time and again.

one

You – a manager?

The majority of this part is targeted at readers who are considering a management career or recently became managers. More experienced managers may want to start the book at the fourth article of this part.

This first part of the book explains the basics. It will help you answer questions like: What is management really about? How do you improve your understanding of management? Is it the right career for you? The answers to these questions are largely personal and individually specific. By reading this part you will be better equipped to answer them for yourself.

The truth is that most people coming into management for the first time have at best a vague idea of what it is all about and are influenced by myths, misconceptions and all sorts of assumptions. The first three sections break down some of the big myths of management, and clarify and challenge some of the common assumptions.

The fourth section looks at different ways in which you can envisage your management role – and how your vision of the role affects what you do and how you do it.

The accidental manager

What is this about and why is it important?

Why do people become managers?

A few people make a deliberate and informed choice to become a manager. But for many, apart from a general aspiration to further their careers, becoming a manager is a relatively uninformed choice. A management job is offered, accepted and plunged into without being understood properly.

To some extent this is unavoidable. Management is one of those things that cannot be fully understood until it is tried. When we try something new, we like to dip our toes in at the shallow end and slowly walk into deeper water. Unfortunately, there is no truly shallow end when it comes to management. Most people find the initial period of being a manager challenging.

This is not an argument for becoming paranoid or stressed about taking a management job. Most people survive the plunge into the deep end. But there are ways of making a more informed choice and ways of making your entry into the profession a little easier.

Objectives for managers

- To make an informed choice to become a manager, as far as practical.
- To have sensible and realistic expectations of your future role.

Common issues in achieving these objectives

- Much of the understanding of management can only come from experience. It cannot be learnt from books or taught in a classroom.

■ The expectations and reality of being a manager are often at variance. This can lead to disappointment and disengagement from the role.

The management guide

Why have you chosen a management career? Is it the next logical step on a grand career plan? Is it because you see it as the opportunity for success and wealth (see pp. 14–18)? Or is it simply because someone more senior has asked you to take a job as a manager? Underlying all of these questions are two more general questions:

■ Do you know what you want from a job?

■ Do you think a management role will provide it or is the route to providing it?

If you are honest, apart from earning a living, the answer to the first question is usually 'no', and the response to the second question is 'I'm not sure'. This is not the ideal way to start your career!

However, many people find successful and happy careers in management. Although management is changing and will continue to change, it is and will remain essential to business. Management still provides an attractive long-term career, albeit a different career from a few decades ago and no doubt in future a different career again. Great opportunities do not come along every day and the offer to become a manager is a great one. My general advice if you are offered a management role is to think about it seriously, and not to turn it down unless you have a *very* good reason.

However, it would be an exaggeration to say that everyone enjoys management or becomes a successful manager. This includes people who are brilliant at their current role. A lot of people are surprised by what being a manager means, and are astonished at how different it is from their previous jobs. So, before you accept the offer, think about it a little. Never think you do not have a choice. You always have a choice whether to accept a role or not. Question yourself: are you the right person to be a manager, and is management right for you?

I am not trying to give you perfect foresight. There is no such thing, and the truth is that you cannot fully understand management and what it is like to be a manager until you have tried it. Most people do not really know what managers do, apart from other managers. And even then there is a great variation between the work of one manager and that of another (see pp. 8–13). So what can you do about this?

Preparing for management

You can read around a bit, in books like this one. You can go on courses, especially those that provide the opportunity for discussion. These help, but only partially. Better still you can observe and talk to practising managers. Best of all, you may get the opportunity to follow a manager around, to act as her shadow. If you do, this is well worth doing.

In talking to other managers, you will meet a few who are wildly enthusiastic and many who are neutral – *it's just a job*. But do not be surprised if you come across cynicism. There are a lot of cynics around. Remember you are not trying to find out what they think of their job. You want to know what their job entails, so you can decide whether *you* will enjoy it and thrive at it.

Additionally, and most importantly, you should develop your self-knowledge. What is it that you really want in life? Is this compatible with being a manager?

The job on offer

So far what I have discussed is relatively generic. But you are not taking any management job. You will be offered a specific management job, one that has its own individual challenges and opportunities. To help understand if it is the job for you, think through the following questions:

- What does this role entail? Will it utilise skills you have or want to develop?
- What are the conditions this work requires you to accept? Are they conditions you are prepared to consent to?
- What is the culture and environment of this role like? Is it a culture and environment you will thrive in?
- What resources will you get? How far can you shape the job as you see fit?
- Why is there an opportunity? Is this a new role, or are you inheriting someone else's team? What are the implications?
- If you are inheriting someone else's team: what challenges does that present? What happened to the previous incumbent and what are the implications?

If you are interested not just in a job, but also in a longer-term career, there are other important aspects of a job to consider. Three areas are particularly important:

- *Learning*: there are useful and less useful things to learn, but generally the more you learn the more valuable you will become. The longevity of your career depends on your ability to learn new things, and therefore your access to learning opportunities. Does this role offer the opportunity to learn? Can you enhance the role in any way so it does?
- *Opportunities*: is this job a stepping stone to future roles? Promotion may not be on your mind the first day you take a new job, but if you want to progress in your career it is worth thinking about this from the outset.
- *Visibility*: you will not get promoted unless someone decides to promote you. To be promoted you must be visible to more senior managers with the power and desire to promote you. Does this role have sufficient visibility to important stakeholders?

Another thing to consider is that the role will change. Whatever the role is now, it will not be the same in ten or twenty years' time. Your career will move along, and the demands of business will change. For example, my career started in a company making a profitable everyday product which hardly exists any more (film for cameras), working as an expert on a technology platform that no one uses any more, in an organisational structure that has largely gone (everything done in-house in one location – it is now all outsourced globally). I cannot predict what, but I can be sure equally profound changes will happen in your career.

Starting a management career

Perfect information about a role does not exist. The perfect role probably does not exist either. You usually have to accept some degree of compromise. Sooner or later you have to take the plunge and take a management role. If you are going to take the plunge, sooner is probably better.

What happens when you start a management career? Initially you may feel lost and under pressure. A few people stall at the first hurdle, in the first few days, weeks and months of a new role. You need to separate the experience of becoming a manager for the first time from being a manager in the longer run. When you first become a manager prepare yourself for challenging times.

Comfort yourself that everyone goes through this stage and it will not last forever. Often, it is when you are under pressure that you will learn the most important skills and lessons in the quickest way. This may seem like a small recompense, but it is a significant repayment for those initial stresses and strains.

Anticipate that things will not be as you expect. Try to get lots of feedback. Be willing to try different things if what you are doing is not working as you expected. Keep engaging your boss (see pp. 62–7). Is she happy with what you are doing, does she have any advice or tips, are you doing the right things? Observe your peers doing similar jobs, especially the successful ones (see pp. 68–73). What do they do that makes them successful? There is plenty of information if you seek it out.

Set expectations with family and friends that you will be under pressure for a few months and may be less responsive than usual. Ask for their support and understanding.

What if you are ambitious or competitive? At the start of a career it can be seductive to try and jump some steps and race straight to the highest-profile roles. You should not forget that for most people a career means 40+ years of work. Sometimes the most direct path to the top is not the best way. The hares do not always win the races but may tire out to be overtaken by tortoises going on to achieve greater long-term success. I'm not saying don't be ambitious or jump for that once-in-a-lifetime opportunity. But don't assume it is the best option, and if you don't get it, don't assume that you will never catch up or overtake those who have jumped.

What if it does not work out? Don't decide that management isn't for you too quickly. Initially the work will seem demanding and difficult, but over time it should get easier. If after months and years it really is not getting any clearer or easier, then it is time to think again.

Work on this more if ...

■ You are still not sure whether management is for you or not. Remember – some time you will have to make a choice with limited information.

Manager's checklist

■ Seek out relevant information before accepting a management role. Is management right for you? Is this specific role on offer the right one for you?

■ Do not worry if initially it is challenging. Everyone goes through this. See it as an opportunity to learn quickly.

The things managers do

What is this about and why is it important?

What do managers do? What should you do? Simple but surprisingly hard questions to answer.

To choose a job you will excel in and enjoy you need to know what you are letting yourself in for. Unfortunately, it is not clear to most people what being a manager really means. The answer might seem to lie in a list of the things managers do. However, such a list is of limited value. Each management role is unique and you are unique. The answer is to recognise how you can gain and maintain a full understanding of *your* management role.

Objectives for managers

- To have realistic expectations of new management roles.
- To find a way to explore, discover and create the role that is right for you.
- To develop a clear understanding of the specific role you need to perform to be successful.

Common issues in achieving these objectives

- New managers do not have clear ideas of what being a manager means or entails. They are often surprised and stressed when the job starts. Usually this is a temporary state, but for some managers this leads to disillusionment and disappointment.
- Promotion to management is typically dependent on past performance. Yet a management role entails different activities and requires different skills from your previous role.
- Managers change roles or jobs regularly. Even experienced managers can struggle with new roles.

The management guide

A long time ago it was simple. The manager was *the* boss, often the business owner. What he said, and it almost always was he, went. The boss had power. He ruled and the workers did what he told them to do. The manager bossed around the same group of workers until retirement or death. If anyone had higher education it was the boss, and this was rare – and training in being a manager or running a business was non-existent. If you had asked anyone what the boss did, they would have given you a consistent answer along the lines above.

Well, that's the image anyway. We can find many faults in that picture, but at least it was clear who did what. Some people, usually those who have never worked in a business, still think it is like this. It is not. Real life has continuously migrated away from this image. Modern management bears little resemblance to this picture.

So what is it like now? The manager is almost certainly not the owner – and if she or he is then it is probably a very small company. The workers won't just do what the manager tells them to do. The manager has limited power and must develop influence to get things done. The workers are often significantly more experienced and understand their roles as experts better than the manager does. Although there are exceptions, the manager's tenure in a role is at best a few years, sometimes less. The manager may have a degree, and even a business degree – but then so might all of the workers. And, we don't call the workers 'workers' any more! If you ask a range of people what managers do – you will get a hugely diverse set of answers.

The term *manager* refers to an incredibly varied range of roles. This is made more complex by the use of the word *manager* both to define a role and as a job title. In most cases, someone with the title *manager* has the role of being a manager, but not always. The word *manager* can be affixed to a job title as an honorific label without any management responsibilities, but some, possibly modest, level of seniority. On the other hand, not everyone who performs the role has the job title. People who functionally work as managers can have all sorts of titles such as *team leader, department head* or *director*. This book is aimed at people who function as managers – not those who just happen to have the word *manager* in their title.

Given the range of roles the word *manager* can be applied to, are there common features to the work of all managers? The philosopher Wittgenstein referred to words having *family resemblance*. By this he meant that words refer to things which are related by a series of overlapping similarities, rather than one fundamental common feature. The word *manager* seems to fall into this category. However, we can pick out some features which are common, if not universal, to being a manager:

- Managers are not employed for what they achieve themselves, but for getting things done via other resource in the organisation. *Other resource* usually means a team of people. The team the manager manages. Of course, managers have to do things, such as deciding who does what, helping their team members, and budgeting. But these are means rather than ends or results.

- Historically managers had power inherent in their position which enabled them to instruct the team what to do. To an extent this still works, but it is increasingly unreliable as:

  - Team members in modern society are skilled, educated, opinionated and mobile. They have high expectations and are not frightened to express them. Employees do not expect to be only instructed what to do. Employees need to be motivated, influenced and convinced to perform their work – and consulted on many management decisions.

  - Managers often have cross-functional and processes responsibilities. This requires the management of a network of people – many of whom do not 'work' for the manager. Some may not even be employed in the same organisation. Networking, influencing and political skills are critically important.

■ How managers are measured is typically complex, subjective, ambiguous and changeable.

Depending on the situation, managers may do a whole host of other things. For example, some, but not all, managers do some of the work of the team, act as a subject matter expert, run administrative processes (e.g. budgets, HR), check compliance, are their boss's personal resource to call on, drive change. The manager has to engage, encourage and motivate staff. The manager communicates and leads. The manager finds resources and creates an environment in which a team can perform. The list goes on and on. In fact, two of the core challenges for modern managers are:

■ Making sense of what is on the list of things to do.

■ Determining how to fit it all into the constraint of the time available.

For most people what managers generally do is less relevant than the answer to the question *what do I need to do in my specific management role*? The unhelpful but honest answer is   that depends on the situation. The follow-on question is *how can I find out*?

There are lots of sources of information on your role. For example:

■ *Job specifications*: most organisations provide job specifications. They are useful indications of roles. But they are rarely complete and they tend to be static. The real role of a manager changes dynamically.

■ *Competency frameworks*: many organisations support job specifications with definitions of the competencies required by managers. These are useful, but tend to indicate how your performance will be assessed more than how to do your job.

■ *Your boss*: a good source of information is simply to ask your boss. But bosses are notoriously inconsistent and provide conflicting information on what they require.

■ *Peers*: your peers can be a good source of information about your role. Their opinions are valuable, but they are only opinions. They do not do your job.

■ *Observation*: a great way of improving your understanding is to observe what managers do (as opposed to relying on what they say they do). It is useful to observe successful managers. Sometimes you can get the chance to shadow one. If you do, grab it.

These sources of information are, at best, partial descriptions of the role. They are pieces of a jigsaw puzzle. All such data needs to be treated with care. The sources are incomplete and often wrong. For instance, ask many people if their role relates to their documented job specification, and the answer is often – *vaguely at best* or *it did 2 years ago when I took the job, but not now.*

Your role has to be explored and discovered. To some extent, and often a significant extent, you create your own management role.

In reality, it is impossible to understand your role fully until you have performed it for some time. You must expect to develop your understanding of what is required and what is important as you experience the role. On top of this, your job will naturally modify over time. To succeed as a manager you must be willing to observe and listen, to learn, to monitor performance and to regularly seek feedback. There will be an element of experimentation as well as trial and error. This requires a level of resilience in you as an individual.

One of the main aims of this book is to help you develop this understanding. Parts 2 and 3 focus specifically on this.

Now, there is one problem with this that the reader may have spotted. If you don't know completely what your role is until you are doing it, *how can you be certain it is right for you?* This is the nature of management work. You may see this as unfortunate, uncomfortable or troubling. Alternatively, you can see this as positive, exciting, challenging and offering the opportunity to shape the role to yourself.

Work on this more if ...

■ You don't know what managers do. You think you may be focusing on the right activities, missing out critical activities, or prioritising sub-optimally between different aspects of the role.

■ You are insufficiently dynamic in terms of regularly modifying your role or priorities as needs change.

Manager's checklist

■ There is not one universal definition of management. Managers perform a wide range of roles. There are sources of information, such as job definitions, which help to create a picture. The information needs to be treated with care as it is incomplete and may even be wrong.

■ However well informed you are when you take on a role, you will not understand it fully until you have experienced it for some time. You must explore, discover and then create your role as a manager.

■ To excel you must monitor performance, seek regular feedback and regularly modify and improve what you do as a manager.

Success, happiness and the management career

What is this about and why is it important?

There is an unstated assumption in many books, courses and conversations on management. It is an assumption that is worth making explicit and challenging. The assumption has two parts. These are:

- if you are good as a manager you will have a successful career;
- if you are successful you will be happy.

These are statements that have been and are true for some people in management roles. But as universal points, they are blatantly false. We all know they are false when they are stated like this, but usually they are left as hidden and implicit conjectures. As such they can be highly misleading.

Objectives for managers

- To understand how management can lead to personal success and happiness.
- To understand the risks and limitations of a management career.

Common issues in achieving these objectives

- Many people do not know what they want in life.
- There is a tendency to a simplistic judgement of success as deriving from rewards, predominantly money and status.

The management guide

Are managers successful? Are managers happy? Most people would agree that these are fairly meaningless questions. But there are two more relevant questions: will you be successful and will you be happy in a management career? A book cannot answer these questions for you, but I can make some observations which may help you answer them.

It is a matter of fact that some managers are extremely successful. Read the financial or business pages in the press and see the latest CEO pay rises. It's not hard to find managers who receive rewards and benefits that are beyond most people's dreams. If your measure of success is rewards and money – these people are successful. Some managers have huge amounts of power and control – as much resource as a small country. If your measures of success are status and influence – then these managers have it. The important word in all of these sentences is *some*. Perhaps I should really have used the phrase *a few*.

Many managers are content and make a reasonable living. If you become a manager, do the job well, and constantly learn new skills so you can adjust as business needs adapt, the chances are you will do quite well and continue to do quite well. But there are two uncomfortable truths for anyone who is looking to management as the road to fortune and happiness:

- For most managers, a management career is not the route to the highest financial rewards.
- Great management skills do not always lead to the most senior roles within business.

There are many aspects to rewards, as I will discuss on pp. 109–115. But what often jumps into people's minds, when the word *reward* is uttered in a professional context, is money. Whilst considering rewards only in financial terms is blinkered, money is a very important aspect of most people's careers. So, for now, let's consider finance. What careers can offer better financial rewards than management? Without too much effort I can think of several careers:

- *Entrepreneurs* – most of the people who have made serious fortunes are entrepreneurs. To become a successful entrepreneur, running a large enterprise, you may need to develop management skills, but your primary skill is being an entrepreneur. If that is what you want to be – go out and do it. A management career in a business is something quite different. Of course, as an entrepreneur you may also lose everything, whereas as a manager this is unlikely.

■ *Entertainers and sports stars* – probably more difficult and certainly less likely than becoming a successful manager. But if you do make it you will earn orders of magnitude more than most managers.

■ *Professional services* – senior lawyers, accountants and management consultants earn far more than most managers. Whilst they may be constantly travelling and working long hours, they often have a significantly less stressful life than many managers. One source of this limited stress is the small size of teams and the comparatively simple line management challenge.

■ *Sales person* – yes, there are sales people toiling away earning a pittance. But in many organisations, especially those selling to other businesses or governments, some of the highest-paid people are the people who sell. If you want to earn a lot of money quickly, go into sales. Many sales people actively avoid management careers, and businesses can struggle to get their best sales people to become sales managers.

If you are reading this book, I assume either you are a manager and you want to stay a manager, or you want to start a career in management. It may not be the only route or even the most certain route to success, but it is the one that suits you and you want to follow it.

The good news is that some of the most successful people in business are brilliant managers. Some people are successful because of their management skills. The less welcome news is that there is not a perfect correlation between brilliance as a manager and a successful career. I have met many successful people, in very senior roles in organisations, who are terrible managers. I have also met many brilliant managers toiling away for the whole of their career at the base of an organisation.

Why is there a gap? Firstly, there is plain old good luck. We cannot deny the existence of luck. Like it or not, some people just get lucky. The world is random and these things happen. Don't knock it. One day something lucky will happen to you – you will be in the right place at the right time. Seize the opportunity when it happens – it won't happen often. The other side of this point is that some people are sometimes unlucky. If unlucky things happen, all you can do is get over it and keep pushing on. Either way, do not focus on how lucky or unlucky you have been as it leads to negative and defeatist thinking.

Secondly, and more importantly, successful people manage their job to be successful (see pp. 213–18). If you want to have a successful career you have to work at being successful. Successful people are successful not just because they are good at what they do, but because they plan and take actions that help their career. Examples include:

- Making sure achievements at work are visible to people who matter.
- Developing networks and focusing those networks on people whom they can help and who can help them.
- Choosing roles carefully – only taking those that help their careers.
- Occasionally taking risks, and being the (lucky?) ones whom the risks pay off for.

You might be thinking at this stage: so why bother with improving your management skills? You should bother because your management career will be more rewarding. Being a better manager will make you more likely to have a better career. You increase your chances of being one of the few who have huge success based on management skills. Finally, you should bother because if you are in a management role, your life will be easier and more pleasant if you are good at it.

So far, all I have talked about is success. What about happiness? We can define success in terms of being happy. But I will avoid that as the word *success* has been hijacked and tends to mean financial success, fame and status – and we are all well aware of the fact that these are not the same as happiness. Of course, material possessions and an ability to pay your bills help many people to have a less stressful life, or to feel they are successful, and this can lead to happiness. But happiness is a more complex and elusive beast than this. Some components of happiness are:

- Knowing what makes you happy – and striving for that ahead of anything else.
- Avoiding what makes you unhappy – and staying clear of it if you can.
- Calmly accepting those things that you cannot change or influence.

Fundamentally, as long as you are not in a state of distress such as pain or hunger, happiness is an attitude. It is a choice. You can choose it any time you want. This may or may not have anything to do with management. But if you are going to be a manager, ideally it should be something that makes you happy. If not, it is the wrong choice for you. If you want to be a manager, you might as well choose to be a happy manager.

Work on this more if ...

- You are not sure if what you want in life and what a management career offers are aligned.

Manager's checklist

- There is not a direct correlation between success and management skills.
- If you want to be successful, you not only have to be good at what you do, you need to manage your career to be successful.
- Great management skills are worth striving for. They will increase the likelihood of success and your enjoyment of your job.

Picturing your role

What is this about and why is it important?

Each manager has unique thought processes about their role. These thought processes form a mental model. Everyone has mental models, not just managers, and not just about management roles. But they are particularly important for managers to be aware of, as they have a significant effect on the effectiveness of a manager.

Mental models affect managers' performance, especially with regard to those things that are done intuitively. They help in scoping management roles – the work an individual manager chooses to do and chooses to overlook. Mental models are used in reasoning and decision making. Such models also act as information filters – determining what information is perceived and analysed and which information is ignored.

It is a very simplistic definition, but you can think of a mental model as an internal picture of your role. This picture is subconscious most of the time. It can be a significant and unwelcome surprise when something happens that challenges your mental model. The picture formed depends on your personality, your experiences, how you think – and, critically, the assumptions you make about the world. There is no right and wrong when it comes to mental models, but some are more helpful in certain situations than others.

Mental models enable managers to interpret the world efficiently, and can help managers to perform their roles effectively. But mental models can also limit you. For example, if your mental model does not envisage certain necessary aspects of the management role then you are likely to miss these out, with detrimental effects on your management performance.

It can be difficult to adapt your mental model, especially the central aspects that derive from the core assumptions you make about the world. But mental models are not static and it is possible to deliberately change them. In this section, I want to challenge you to think consciously about your personal picture of the manager's role.

Don't just go through this section once. Come back to the points made here when you have completed the book, and return to them time and again. For new managers this may be more challenging as you may not have formed a mature mental model. The sooner you start to think about creating a model the better.

Objectives for managers

■ To be able to picture the role of a manager from different perspectives.

■ To be able to adapt mental models to different situations and circumstances.

■ To see if your mental model is limiting your management performance, so you can modify it if necessary.

Common issues in achieving these objectives

■ Building a mental model from a set of inappropriate assumptions.

■ Being unable to make your mental model explicit, even to yourself.

■ Becoming stuck with a model that has worked well in one situation, but which is less effective in others.

The management guide

This section consists of lists of statements and questions to help clarify your current images of management. The aim is to open your thinking to alternative pictures. The intention is not to identify if a model is right or wrong. Models are not things the terms *right* and *wrong* apply to. But models can be more or less appropriate and more or less effective for a specific context and situation.

This section is not an exhaustive or comprehensive analysis of mental models. This would probably take a whole book in itself. But it is a wide-ranging list of points. Read through the list and challenge yourself to think about the questions asked here.

We will look at the role of the manager from five different perspectives:

1. What is a successful manager?
2. How do you contribute to achieving the team's outcome?
3. What is your relationship with your team members?
4. How do you ensure the team delivers?
5. What is your relationship with the rest of the organisation?

For each of these perspectives read the associated statements and see if any of them reflect your current views. Consider if you would be more effective and successful if you adopted a different view.

What is a successful manager?

A successful manager:

■ Runs a well-functioning part of the organisation, e.g. *I am an integral part of the finance function.*
■ Completes work, e.g. *I make sure my team gets all the billing done.*
■ Manages a process, e.g. *I run the order to cash process.*
■ Achieves an outcome, e.g. *We get the revenues in.*
■ Enhances value, e.g. *My team regularly reduces debtor days and improves our cash position.*
■ Develops people, e.g. *My team members constantly learn new skills.*

How do you contribute to the team's outcome?

■ Are you a full-time manager or do you also do some of the team's work? *I am the captain* or *I am a player–manager.*

- Are you a subject-matter expert or are you an expert manager? *People should come to me when they really need specialist advice* or *I rely on my team members' skills and my job is to manage them.*
- Are you part of a team or part of management? *I'm just one of the lads* or *I ensure they work in the way required.*

What is your relationship with your team members?

- I am the boss. *I am the top of a pyramid.*
- I am one layer in the hierarchy. *I'm in my team, and part of my boss's team too.*
- I'm a spider in a web. *I see the organisation as a network of relationships including my team and others in the organisation.*
- I'm my team members' friend and protector. *I make sure they get their entitlements – nobody messes around with my team.*
- I'm a gatekeeper. *I manage access to my team as a pool of resource.*

How do you ensure the team delivers?

- I am task-focused. *I decompose the overall task into activities for individuals, prioritise and allocate work, and monitor and chase progress.*
- I enable the team to work. *I make decisions, fix problems, remove barriers, and generally permit the team to do what they need to do.*
- I am a boundary setter. *I provide general direction and guidelines to the team and define the overall scope of the team members' work.*
- I am a gatekeeper. *I give permissions and provide or deny access to resources.*
- I am an environment builder. *I create the system and situation in which the team can be productive.*
- I am a sense maker. *I take in relevant information, structure and analyse it, and create the picture of the world for the team.*

- I am a communicator and translator. *I take in ideas and information from across the organisation and explain it to the team. This gives context and direction to their work.*
- I am a role model. *I personally exhibit ideal behaviour for team members to copy.*
- I am a facilitator and coach. *I help team members to grow and develop to better perform their role and achieve their individual goals.*

What is your relationship with the rest of the organisation?

- Where do you focus? *Do you focus into the team or out to the rest of the organisation?*
- Are you task- or process-focused? *Do you do your job as best you can, or think how best your job fits into the wider picture?*
- How is the organisation structured? *Do you see a hierarchy, silos, processes or a network?*
- How influential do you try to be? *Do you just respond to the business's strategy or do you also influence the agenda?*
- What relationships are important? *Suppliers, customers, peers, hierarchy, or other stakeholders?*

Work on this more if ...

- You cannot determine why you are not achieving as much as other managers.
- You have a static and restricted view of your role as a manager.
- You find the questions in the lists above difficult to answer.

Manager's checklist

- Do not get fixated on one single image of your role. Try to flex it to the situation and over time.
- Try and make your mental model explicit to yourself and be willing to modify it when it no longer achieves your objectives.

two

The team

In the first part we learnt about the role of the manager.
In later parts we will explore how to execute that role.
This part discusses the focal point for all management
attention – your team. Teams are the reason there are
managers, and the vehicle through which managers
achieve their goals.

The primary aim of management is to influence team
members to take the right actions. To be able to do this
you need to understand how your personal style affects
people, and how you can best influence team members to
do what is needed.

This part looks at assembling teams and developing your
understanding of what a team wants, and raises your
awareness of the changing structure of teams. It starts
with an exploration of your personal style of interaction.

The team starts with you

What is this about and why is it important?

When you become a manager an interesting thing happens. You expect to become more in control of your own destiny, but you turn out to be *more dependent* on other people. Your core dependency is on the individuals in your team. If they perform well, you achieve your goals. If they perform badly, you fail. What you personally achieve matters little. What matters is what the team as a whole achieves.

Yet the team starts with you. How well the team functions is significantly affected by the role you take, the ways you interact with individuals and the relationships you develop with them. You may worry about the quality of the people in your team. This is important, but you should also think about yourself. A team made up of brilliant individuals will perform poorly with a poor manager. But a team of moderately competent individuals can perform exceptionally with a brilliant manager.

How do you get team members to do things? The easy answer is to use power. *I am a manager and I exert management power to get things done.* New managers are often disappointed at how small their power is in reality. Positional power is useful for managers, but successful managers rely on it to a relatively small degree. This is for two reasons: in reality, usually you don't have that much power, and even when you do it is not the most effective way to achieve your goals. Successful managers know how to influence people without resorting to power. To a large degree management is influencing.

The management power that exists is useful for people who directly report to you. With greater inter-functional and cross-process work, and the use of virtual and project teams, managers have to spend more and more time getting people who do not report to them to do things. If someone does not work for you, your positional power is largely irrelevant. What is important is your ability to influence people.

You influence people by your deliberate actions: what you ask people to do, how you ask them, the relationships you choose to develop. But you also influence people in less conscious ways – by the ways you behave and interact on a day-to-day basis.

Objectives for managers

- To understand how your personal style affects people.
- To develop powerful influencing skills.

Common issues in achieving these objectives

- Over-reliance on positional power.
- Lack of self-awareness.
- Unwillingness to seek and respond to feedback.

The management guide

Power comes from many sources – position, expertise and relationships are common sources. As a manager you have power inherent in your position. For instance, you can determine pay and rewards. These seem powerful and useful levers. The underlying bargain with a member of staff is of the forms: *if you do this, I will ... if you don't do this, I will ...* There are, however, several good reasons for not relying on these levers.

Firstly, they don't always work. Even with power individuals still sometimes refuse to do the things you ask. You may utilise a carrot or a stick. But what happens if they still refuse? In terms of the goals you need to achieve, all recourse to such power means is that something has not happened. You only succeed if your team performs well. There is no reward for how many sticks or carrots you have applied.

Secondly, your ability to use these levers is constrained. For instance, unless you are quite senior in an organisation your ability to hand out significant differentials in pay rises is very limited. An extra 1% for someone who is performing well is not much of a motivation.

Thirdly, even when it works, relying on power is not the best means of developing a productive team. Constantly calling on positional power leads to a confrontational relationship. Such relationships are rarely, if ever, productive. With increasing education and changes in social aspirations people do not expect, and may not put up with, confrontation or command-and-control styles of relationships with their managers. They expect managers to guide them, not order them.

Fourthly, it's not much fun if everything staff need to do has to be bargained for. You will have a much more pleasant life if people do the things you ask them to do without constant threats or offers of reward. You may be a manager for decades, and you should think about what will make it enjoyable.

The alternative to positional power is to develop and use your influence. Influence is the way you produce an effect on the actions, decisions or beliefs of other people. (Closely associated with influence is motivation, see pp. 109–15.) The interesting thing about influence is that once you develop sufficient influence *it becomes power*. If your influence is visible it will affect people's judgement of you. The simple fact that you are known to have influence will make you more and more influential.

Even very smart managers sometimes fail to rely enough on influence. This is because it is not pure intelligence that makes great managers. It is the ability to interact productively with individuals and teams, interpret situations, politics and inter-personal dynamics, and influence people. Daniel Goleman identified this when he coined the phrase *emotional intelligence* in his book of the same name (Bantam Books, 2006). (Emotional intelligence is usually abbreviated to EI, or sometimes referred to as Emotional Quotient or EQ.)

Of course, a high IQ is a wonderful and useful thing. But unless you understand and know how to work with people and have sufficient EI, you will not get anywhere as a manager. This seems intuitively right, as we all know at least one ultra-smart person who struggles with social interaction and dealing with people. Such a person may have many virtues, but would be a poor manager – not knowing how to influence people.

Some managers suffer from the slightly different problem of being fixed with one influencing style. One influencing style is not sufficient. You need to be able to interact differently with various groups of stakeholders. In different situations you want to create distinct responses. To create a distinct response requires a specific type of interaction.

Influencing skills are a result of your emotional intelligence. But you should not think you have a fixed quotient of emotional intelligence. Some people naturally have greater EI than others – however, with effort you can improve your EI. You can get ideas how to do this from reading, and be helped by coaching.

The goal for all managers is to develop positive relationships. I do not mean friendships, but the type of relationship where you can get things done, you are listened to and are influential, and where you gain access to the resources you need. What sorts of styles of interaction help? This is context- and culture-specific. The influencing skills required to deal with a high-pressure problem requiring immediate resolution are different from those required in developing a well-thought-through design for a long-term issue. How you interact with some senior professional specialists, for instance lawyers, may need to be different from dealing with a supplier delegation. What is appropriate in a Western European context is often different from that required in an Asian setting.

Consider two managers who ask their team members to perform a task. What makes one more effective than the other? For a start it's not just what he asks, but *how* he asks. More importantly, it's not just about asking. It is also about relationships, expectations and the judgements people have already made about the individual manager. These are derived from experiences with and observations of the day-to-day behaviour of each manager.

Your ability to influence people is dependent on their judgements of you. As a manager, you are being constantly judged by your team. All of your actions affect this judgement. The big decisions you make and the way you communicate them affect judgements. But it is your everyday behaviour that affects people's judgement of you most: how you walk into the office in the morning, how often you smile, your humour, the trust you show in team members, your level of enthusiasm, your responses to unacceptable behaviour and poor performance, and how often you make positive comments and so on.

It is important that you start to develop an understanding of how your normal behaviour and style of interaction affects people. Do you know what reaction you generally cause in other people?

Developing great influencing skills depends on self-awareness. Self-awareness comes from observation, listening and feedback from others. If you never ask for feedback, the only information you have on your influence is your own perception. Your perception is subjective and biased. When it comes to influencing it is other people's views and beliefs that are important. Improved influencing skills come from a willingness to act on feedback and to change the way you behave and interact with people.

If you want to improve your influence and your relationships get some feedback. Asking for feedback is not always easy, and sometimes you may not have the confidence to do it. Therefore start by asking people you know and trust, for example family members and friends. *How did I come across in that situation? How did I make you feel? What could I have done differently?* Make clear you do not want confidence-boosting platitudes or being told that they like you. You need constructive criticism so you can improve in influencing a wide variety of people.

Accepting feedback on how people perceive your behaviour can be one of the most difficult things to do. It can feel threatening and hurtful. So, prepare yourself for some painful information.

Don't let this put you off. After a while seeking feedback becomes natural and less difficult to do. If you get feedback every day it stops feeling like criticism and starts becoming just useful information to think about.

Work on this more if ...

- You rely solely on your power as a manager to get things done.
- You are not aware of how your personal style affects people.
- You are regularly in conflict with team members.
- You are ineffective in achieving team goals through your team members.

Manager's checklist

- Do not rely on power to fulfil your management role.
- Work to develop the ability to influence people to do as you ask.
- Observe and listen to how people respond to you. Regularly seek feedback.
- Analyse feedback and adapt your behaviour according to it.

Assembling the team

What is this about and why is it important?

One of the first things managers in new roles must do is to assemble a team. This is often a chaotic time, as a manager in a new role will be under all sorts of pressures.

There are demands to move immediately forward with work. This cannot be done until the team has been assembled and is functioning properly. Third-party expectations have to be managed. Somehow you need to balance the amount of work you promise to do, the amount the business wants you to do and the time to assemble the team. Not all organisations are patient and will give a manager much breathing space to assemble their teams.

Additionally, unless you have been promoted to a management role from within the team, your understanding of what the team is required to do will be limited. Hence there is a risk you will assemble the wrong team. Improving on your understanding of the team's role and objectives usually takes some time (see Part 3).

The temptation for a manager can be to respond to the pressure and assemble a team as quickly as possible. But the decisions you make now, including the choices about who will be in the team, will have long-term implications for you and your performance. A quickly assembled team is usually not the optimal team.

Objectives for managers

- To build an effective team.
- To develop productive relationships with the team members.
- To meet the expectations of key stakeholders.

Common issues in achieving these objectives

- When you start a new role your understanding of the team's task and the capabilities of individuals is limited.
- Getting to understand tasks and capabilities takes time, but there is pressure to move ahead quickly.
- There are constraints on your freedom to pick and choose the people you want, and the scale of resources you would like.

The management guide

When you take on a new management position there are two urgent objectives for you:

- To develop a sufficiently accurate understanding of your role.
- To assemble the resources to fulfil this role.

Other parts of this book are concerned with developing an understanding of your role. In this section, I look at assembling the main resource to fulfil your role – your team. There are essentially two situations you can find yourself in: inheriting a team and building a new team. We will look at the difference between those situations, but to begin with I will make some general points about assembling your team.

Do not imagine you can assess the situation so accurately that you can assemble the perfectly sized team. There is never enough information to create a perfectly accurate demand plan (see pp. 167–72). Even if you could, it would only be true at the point it was created and within days it will cease to be accurate. You have to assume some variation in workload. Whilst logic might tell you to understand your workload and then size the team, often what you end up doing is working out how big your team budget is and then managing expectations as to the workload this size of team can handle.

You rarely have the time or are in the situation to build the team you want. There will always be compromises, and there will usually be limits to the level of control you have over team choices. Compromise is reality. But rather than taking every compromise, identify the compromises you will accept and the ones you are unwilling to accept. Partially, this is about making decisions within the constraints imposed on you, but it is also about deciding which battles you are going to fight.

You cannot fight every battle. You do not have the time, and if you argue over everything it can damage your relationship with important stakeholders. However, you must fight some battles. For example, what is the minimum budget or team size that you can work with? If you are offered some difficult staff with known performance problems – do you really want to take them? If not, these are battles worth fighting.

Whilst assembling the team you must constantly manage the expectations of your key stakeholders. You have been given a new role. You are being watched and judged. You want to impress your new boss and important customers. However, try and manage expectations downwards and resist the temptation to make grand promises about what you will achieve, at least in the short run. Successful managers are masters at managing expectations. A high-performing team takes time to build, and you need to give yourself time to build it.

The inherited team

In the situation when you are taking over an existing team, your most important immediate task is to keep the team performing. No one wants to see a dip in performance just because a new manager has taken over. Your boss certainly won't. There is also a less urgent, but in the longer term more important task: to decide what, if anything, needs to change. Do not leave this decision too long. Within a few months you should be in a position to know the scale and type of changes you want to make.

The decision of what, if anything, to change depends on a range of factors: history, expectations, your understanding of the situation, and your management style. Already, there may be expectations about what you will do, or even promises made during your selection. Find out quickly what commitments your boss has made.

One of the most useful things to understand is why there was a team for you to inherit. Was the previous incumbent promoted (is he now your boss)? Did he move on? Was he pushed? When you know the answers you can work out the implications for you and what you need to do.

Don't change things for the sake of it. There is no need as a new manager to stamp your identity on a team just because you are a new manager. If you understand the situation fully, and are a confident expert, change away as you see fit. However, if you have a limited understanding as you come into a role, leave it as it is until you understand better.

Get to know your workload. Observe, talk and listen to team members. Assess their performance. Ask your peers who run departments your team interacts with for advice. Make sure you know what your boss likes and dislikes about the team.

If you decide that you need to change some of the people in the team, prepare yourself for a long piece of work. Swapping people around takes time. Performance management processes are generally onerous and slow-moving.

As a manager you will feel it is your role to judge the team, but coming into an already existing team it is you who will be judged. First impressions are hard to change – and therefore try to create the right first impressions with your team.

It is always worth remembering that an inherited team needs team building. When you become the manager the team has changed and needs to be built again.

The new team

The challenge with a new team is very different from that with the inherited team. Theoretically, you can select the people you want. The immediate job is to understand the goals your team is intended to meet. From this you can identify the type of resources and the scale of resources required. The second task is to build or recruit the team, and usually there is pressure to build the team quickly.

There are lots of important factors in recruiting or assembling a new team, but there are some essential principles to try and stick to.

Firstly, always go for quality of people over quantity of staff. If there is a big workload the temptation can be to staff up with lots of people. If you need lots of people then go and get them. But higher-quality team members will be more productive than lower-quality – sometimes several times as productive. Also, a higher-quality, smaller team will be easier to manage.

However, do not assume that recruiting people with A-star CVs will get you the best team. Many organisations have an obsessive focus on individual talent. There are some professions in which the success of the team is simply the success of the individual players. In that case individual excellence is what you are after. But in most professions the team is more than the individuals, or at least it should be. Therefore you are not looking for individual excellence – you are looking for excellent team members.

Some team members may need very specific and specialist skills. However, generally attitude is more important than specific skills. Of course, a candidate needs the capability to learn, but I would always rather have a keen and willing team member who wants to and can learn, than an unmotivated and self-important expert. It is generally easier to learn new skills than to change the attitude of people.

If you can avoid quickly pinning down your exact resource profile and leave some headcount for later recruitment, do this. It is only after you have done the work for a while that you will really understand what is required. A little flexibility will help you. However, don't leave it too long as budgets have a habit of being squeezed. Unfilled headcount may disappear from your budget.

Recruit the right people rather than recruit quickly. If you recruit too quickly and just take who you can find, you will often repent in the longer run. If you need someone quickly, hire a contractor for 3–6 months whilst you find the right people.

Who is the team? Which team are you in?

A team may be larger than the people who report to you. As well as your direct reports you may be a part of cross-functional, process and project teams. Modern organisational structures and the tendency for outsourcing make team boundaries blurred (see pp. 45–51). Additionally, you are dependent on a range of other functions in the organisation (see pp. 101–6). You work in a web of interactions and relationships.

Getting your work done is not simply a result of recruiting the right team. Many things you require should be done elsewhere in the organisation. You, and potentially some of your team members, need networking and effective political skills (see pp. 101–6).

Work on this more if ...

- You are starting a new role and you do not know how to assemble the team or what team to assemble.

Manager's checklist

- When you take on a new role manage expectations. Give yourself some breathing space to learn what is required before making too many important decisions.

- When you inherit a team make sure you avoid a performance dip when you take over. Then work out what, if anything, you want to change.

- When you build a new team go for quality over quantity, attitude over skills and the right people rather than the ones you can get quickly.

What does your team want from you?

What is this about and why is it important?

The traditional model of a business has a centralised strategy which cascades down through the organisation. This strategy defines detailed business plans, and is communicated through the layers in the organisational hierarchy. The plans are parcelled out for different aspects to be achieved by separate teams. Managers instruct their teams what to do. Team members follow the instructions because they get paid for it.

This model breaks down if the assumptions it is built on are false. They are.

A detailed strategy which controls everything undertaken in the organisation is a myth. Businesses must respond rapidly and flexibly to local situations and conditions. There may be a common high-level direction, but the details are worked out locally. Staff do not just follow instructions, they make judgements and influence the direction of the business. Empowered staff making critical judgements need to be managed in an appropriate fashion.

No one works just for a salary. The workforce is mobile. There may be easier and more difficult times to change jobs, but your valuable employees have employment options. Salary is only one factor amongst many that makes a job preferable. Your personal style of managing people is critically important. One of the main reasons why people leave organisations is because of the way their managers treat them.

Tenure is also an issue. Often the tenure of the manager is less than that of the staff. You may have moved on to another role, and so may have your successors – yet most of the team may be in the same jobs. They have seen managers come and go. If they do not like your style and direction, team members may keep their heads down and ignore you as you will be gone in 18 months. The painful truth is that they are sometimes right that they can ignore you. Therefore it is important to get team members on your side rather than assuming they will follow you.

You will not become a successful manager just because you have been appointed to a management position. Success depends on your acceptance as a manager by your team. To a significant extent, you will be accepted by your team because you fulfil their expectations of a manager, and you manage the team in the way they feel they should be managed.

Of course, you cannot always manage people in the way they want to be managed. Sometimes you have to make decisions and act in a way team members do not like. But this should not be the primary state of affairs. There are good reasons for acting in a way that team members want:

- Team members will be more responsive to your requests if they feel they are appropriately treated.
- Team members will be more productive and motivated if you are perceived to be fulfilling their needs.
- You are more likely to attract the best candidates if people can see positive reasons to work for you.
- Many of the traits that team members like to see in managers actually lead to good management.

Objectives for managers

- To manage the team in the way that achieves the best possible outcomes.
- To find a personal style of management that accomplishes the above.

Common issues in achieving these objectives

- Lack of understanding of team members' needs and desires.
- Perceiving the team as a resource purely to achieve the manager's goals.

The management guide

You want to be accepted as a manager, to have your thoughts and opinions respected, and your decisions and instructions followed. To achieve this it helps to manage people in a way they feel is appropriate. This may sound like egalitarian nonsense or the road to chaos. It is not. Most people have sensible and reasonable expectations of their manager, and know what is practical and attainable in terms of a working culture.

Team members will respond most positively to managers who exhibit certain characteristics. So what are the traits of a good manager?

Characteristics of a good manager

Everyone has distinct desires. Different organisations have varying cultures which promote specific types of manager, and attract particular types of employee. Therefore it is impossible to document the definitive list of good management traits. But it is possible to give a helpful indication.

The list below shows characteristics that most people tend to like in their managers. You will find individuals who prefer other things, but experience shows this to be a generally valid representation. The list is neither in priority order nor exhaustive.

Being clear Providing clear and understandable goals. People know where they stand as a team and as individuals in that team.

Being consistent A manager who behaves in a consistent and predictable fashion.

Having confidence A manager who is confident without being arrogant. Confidence is not pretending you have answers to all questions, or even know what the questions are. Confidence is the ability to say calmly and without feeling threatened 'I don't know what to do now, any suggestions?'

Being decisive Making the right decisions quickly, and without fuss (see pp. 139–44).

Acting fairly to team members Treating everyone in the team according to the same principles. (But do be partial towards the team – i.e. it is 'fair' to be biased in favour of the team.)

Encouraging fun Work cannot always be fun, but when it is, teams are more productive and staff turnover tends to be lower.

Being honest With honesty comes an ability to believe and trust what the manager says. An example of honesty is the willingness to admit mistakes.

Having influence and being respected Team members like to work with a manager who is influential and respected. They feel it helps them personally, and gives a higher profile to the team.

Valuing learning and development For many people development is critically important. A manager who gives access to learning and development opportunities is appreciated. This can be both formal training and learning on the job. A manager who is a role model who can be learnt from is ideal.

Having a high profile Individuals like to work in a high-profile team that their peers in other teams regard as a good team to be part of.

Being reasonable A balanced manager who makes decisions and requests which people perceive to be reasonable. Reasonableness depends on context. It does not mean you cannot be demanding if the situation requires it.

Gaining resources A manager who gains access to the resources that team members need to do their job.

Giving space to do the job People want space to get on with their job and a feeling their manager trusts them to do it – and even to make mistakes. Team members want help when it is required, but most people do not like someone constantly looking over their shoulder.

Having team members' interest at heart A manager who is not there to simply exert the will of the company, but who fights the team's corner when necessary.

Valuing team members It is a basic human desire to feel valued. Team members will go a long way for a manager who makes them feel valued.

Providing vision A manager who clarifies the role of the team, explains how the team fits with the rest of the business and adds value to it, and makes clear where the team is going. It is worth remembering that teams do not necessarily expect grand or innovative visions.

If you ask what sort of manager people like to work for, the word *leader* comes up frequently. People prefer to work for what they define as *leaders*. This is not a terribly helpful statement, as what team members perceive as good leadership is highly variable. If someone says this, it is worth exploring what they mean in more detail.

Make use of the traits you naturally have. If you do not exhibit them, try to develop them, but do not worry if you are not perfect. Few managers exhibit all of these traits.

Let your team members regularly give you feedback on what they like and dislike about your management style. This does not challenge your position: you can choose to accept or reject the feedback. But it provides excellent information to help improve your management skills.

Undesirable traits from the team's viewpoint

There are many negative traits which teams obviously don't want. For instance, teams don't want a manager who is a bully, a devious manipulator or someone who only cares about himself. But there are some less obvious approaches which managers may think individuals like, but which team members tend not to. Two primary examples are:

- ■ *Everybody's friend*. Team members are happy to work for a friendly manager, but generally they are not looking for a manager to be their personal friend. Team members often need to feel some distance from their manager. Be helpful and supportive, but don't expect to become everyone's buddy.

- ■ *The manager who instinctively knows everyone's desires.* If you assume you know what is in the best interest of team members without asking them, you will get it wrong. A common example is a redundancy situation. It is easy to assume no one wants to be made redundant. For long-serving members of staff, or those with skill sets in demand, the redundancy terms may be more attractive than staying on.

Not surprisingly, team members resent any biases or negative stereotypes held by a manager. In reality, team members themselves are not universally great examples of unbiased behaviour. You will find team members holding all sorts of views based on stereotypes. You should not.

Explicit biases are frowned on in modern society. Biases and stereotypes are best avoided for a number of reasons: many are offensive, unethical or illegal (e.g. racism, sexism, ageism). Additionally, on a purely practical basis, if you are biased against any specific profile of people you are cutting yourself off from a valuable pool of talent.

What if you cannot apply the positive characteristics?

Real life is not about always giving people what they want. You cannot always exhibit positive characteristics. Examples of situations in which you cannot exhibit these traits are:

- From time to time you need to act in a way that may be interpreted to be unfair.
- You cannot always offer learning and development opportunities.
- Sometimes you cannot have the team's interest at heart. As a manager you also represent the organisation's interest, and at times this does not coincide with the team's.
- From time to time you need to be very demanding and this may be seen as unreasonable.
- Occasionally, you may not be able to be completely open and honest. For instance, if a large redundancy programme is about to start you may not be allowed to tell your team until formal announcements have been made.

Also, sometimes team members do have unreasonable or unrealistic desires. A classic example is when team members may feel they should received frequent formal training. Some formal training is expected, but it will be occasional. Most training will be on the job.

How should you handle the situations where you cannot behave as the team desires? As long as you are not constantly at variance with these desires do not worry. Teams do not expect you to be perfect, and will put up with significant amounts of imperfect behaviour from managers. They obviously do, otherwise there would be constant industrial disputes.

If you cannot fulfil the ideal traits at least try to:

- Take the time to explain why you cannot behave in the expected way. Most team members understand that in some situations you have to behave differently.
- Manage expectations. If you expect to behave in a way that is different from normal try to warn the team in advance.
- Modify the team's views. Show the team the value of your way of management. Team members' ideas are not fixed. Over time you can modify their beliefs about what makes a good manager if their experience with you is positive.

Work on this more if ...

- Feedback indicates that team members are dissatisfied with your management style.
- You have higher staff turnover than other managers in similar roles with similar working conditions.

Manager's checklist

- Certain management traits will help you to manage the team better.

- Try to understand the traits the team expects and finds desirable in a manager – and, as far as practical, try to manage in this way.

- However, do not let meeting the expectations or desires of the team get in the way of good management or business outcomes.

The ever-changing shape of the team

What is this about and why is it important?

Teams are evolving.

A manager once had a permanent team in a single office. Now there are geographically spread, virtual and project teams.

Business process re-engineering changed the attention of business value creation from functional excellence to customer-focused process optimisation. From that came cross-functional process teams.

Improvements in technology, globalisation and specialisation enabled outsourcing and offshoring to become commonplace. The team is no longer within a single business.

The Internet has enabled the creation of online communities. Such communities are altering the structure of, and even replacing, the business organisation.

These team types are part of the everyday life of business. Adaptations in the format of teams will continue to proliferate. Innovative team structures provide opportunities for companies – at the same time they create new management challenges. Given their ubiquity, all managers have to be able to deal with these challenges.

Objectives for managers

- To be able to manage a team successfully irrespective of its structure.
- To be able to take advantage of the optimal team structure.

Common issues in achieving these objectives

■ Poor understanding of how to manage different organisational structures effectively.

The management guide

Team types and corresponding management challenges

Let's start with an overview of some of the most common team formats, shown in the table here. The aim is to build a picture of the challenges facing managers from different types of team. The table is not exhaustive, and the types are not mutually exclusive (for instance, an outsourced team may be geographically spread and temporary).

Team type	Description	Sample management challenges
Geographically spread / virtual	Teams working in different locations or time zones – who do not physically meet, but utilise communications technology to coordinate activity and work together	■ Developing relationships without face-to-face contact ■ Explaining and allocating activity ■ Understanding and validating progress without seeing team member outputs
Temporary / task force / project	Teams which exist for a limited duration, and then are disbanded when their goal is achieved. This goal often cuts across the responsibility of multiple managers	■ Limited authority over team members ■ No direct control of the levers for motivation and performance ■ Frequently team members have expertise the manager has no experience of
With more senior team members	Teams (often project teams), of which some of the participants are more senior than the manager running it. For example, a project team with senior experts in it	■ Cannot rely on authority to manage team members of higher seniority

Multi-cultural / multi-lingual	Team with members who do not share a common cultural heritage and norms of behaviour, and may primarily use different languages or variants of language	■ Understanding how to motivate and encourage participation ■ Risk of miscommunication and accidental offence ■ Risk of unaligned sub-teams forming, around cultural or linguistic sub-groups
Cross-organisational	Cross-organisational team, for example one focusing on process performance objectives rather than functional goals	■ Limited authority over team members ■ Interests/goals may not be aligned ■ Mixed loyalties of team members
Peers	Teams, usually temporary, made up of a group of managers of the same seniority	■ Unclear boundaries of responsibility ■ Ego clashes and competition between peers
Voluntary	Teams whose participants are voluntary	■ Limited authority ■ Opinionated and passionate team members who may be less willing to take direction if not agreed with ■ Risk that team members can cease to participate at any time if unhappy
Outsourced / partially outsourced	Team where part of the function or processes are contracted out to a third-party organisation and hence the team crosses organisational boundaries	■ Usually geographically spread ■ Loyalty may be to outsourcing organisation rather than customer firm ■ Manager cannot use normal performance levers to motivate individuals in outsourcing company ■ Can be onerous and time consuming to change/ adapt service due to contract limitations

The principles of successful management

Different types of team need appropriate management. Each places specific pressures on the manager: for example, the amount of travel a manager must undertake. New, currently unforeseen team structures will emerge. As an individual you have little or no ability to influence the emergence and use of these team structures. But to be an effective manager you must be able to deal with them.

However, all is not lost. The principles of successful management remain the same irrespective of the team structure. How you execute and achieve these principles may need to vary, but if you keep yourself focused on these principles you are likely to manage any team structure successfully. Irrespective of the structure you should:

- Know who is in the team, what the objectives are, and what resources are available to achieve these objectives.
- Provide your team members with commonly understood and aligned goals. Each team member must clearly know their role and accountabilities. This is even more important than for a traditional team.
- Clarify roles and expectations of what it will be like to work in the team. *As the manager I am going to ... and I expect you to ... .* Do not assume your view of the manager's role is the same as team members'.
- Develop a shared understanding of the context you are working in. Over time develop a common understanding of the political and stakeholder landscape.
- Try to find objective measures of success. This is not always possible. Many teams have to use subjective, judgemental assessments of success, but objective measures reduce the chance for misunderstanding and misinterpretation.
- Make specific effort to develop relationships and a sense of community in the team. This is harder, but particularly important with geographically spread teams. Get to know individual team members.

- Respect cultural differences. Try to utilise the variations to drive creativity, but minimise divergence in goals or approaches.
- Seek to develop a shared participatory culture. This takes time. Have agreed management mechanisms and styles of working that are common across the team. Try to develop norms of behaviour: for example, what is acceptable to say in the team versus what is acceptable to share outside, and how criticism is given.
- Develop trust. This also takes time, and is a result of your style of interaction and the consistency of your actions. People will not trust managers they are confused by, do not understand or do not have a relationship with.
- Minimise the development of sub-teams and sub-cultures. You are not several teams who come together on a weekly conference call. You are one team. Similarly avoid groups, such as offshore teams, withholding information until it is manipulated into what is perceived as acceptable.

The fundamentals that will determine your management success are: your communication, your behaviour and your actions. The golden rule is: communicate, communicate and communicate again. Communicate as often as possible in the most direct and personalised way possible. This is essential to building shared understanding, shared culture and the development of productive relationships.

If your team is spread, communication becomes a greater burden for the manager. Ideally, have regular face-to-face conversations with all team members. In practice, this is not always possible. When you cannot meet, use communication technology that allows interaction rather than just a push of information outwards. It is through dialogue that relationships develop. Use, but do not rely solely on, periodic conference calls.

Where possible take the time to travel and meet team members. It is feasible to develop relationships with people you have never met, but it is hard. The time and cost investment of meeting team members is usually justified.

If the team is very diverse, keep your language simple and clear. Always check understanding. It is common that people use terminology in different ways, even if they speak the same language.

Avoid location bias. This will lead to cliques and reduce loyalty and trust. Minimise time lags in communicating to remote teams and individuals. Treat everyone the same. Your goal should be to provide the same information, at the same frequency and at the same time to everyone.

By all means use online tools such as social networks, but be careful. Not all team members will be comfortable with or used to them. If you utilise Facebook, LinkedIn or Twitter you must avoid any sense of spying on an individual's private life. As the manager, remember you are more visible than ever before. If you have put any information on the web about yourself, assume someone in your team has seen it.

Work out management mechanisms with your team members. Discuss what helps and what hinders good management. A confident manager is an open manager. And it's not just you who face challenges from the proliferation of teams. Your team members may be in multiple teams. Rather than being their boss you may just be one stakeholder amongst many. If you are competing for attention from your team you will get the best result if you have strong trusting relationships and clear goals.

Beyond the business

Team structures are often moving nowadays beyond the business organisation. Some styles of working together have removed the need for a business altogether. There are online information sources, maintained by volunteers, where once there were paid-for research and information bureaus. Software development was once the preserve of corporations. The phenomenon of shareware has shown the power of communities to develop reliable value-adding tools.

There may be a limit to what such communities of participants can do, but those limits are not yet clear. These are both threats and opportunities for businesses. For the manager who wants to utilise such a community, the ability to understand networks and how to actively engage to develop communities must be a core skill. If you don't have it – go and learn the tools. Don't be afraid to seek advice and training.

In future the need to embrace collaboration and develop participation with people in multiple locations, mixed cultures and languages, and differing types of personal and contractual relationship will increase. This trend will drive the proliferation of organisational structures and team types. New team configurations will arise which have not yet been considered. The manager of the future needs to approach the task of management in a flexible and creative way. Flexibility and creativity will count for more, and extend your career further, than excellence in one management domain.

Work on this more if ...

- You do not understand the different types of team.
- You are faced with a completely different organisational structure than you have worked with before.

Manager's checklist

- The basis for the success of all teams is trusting relationships, clear goals and regular communications.

- You may have to execute your management tasks differently in different types of team, but the principles of good management remain the same.

three

Creating your role

In any business you will find a range of people with differing opinions, goals, skills, resources, views, information, contacts and so on. In its entirety this makes up the human and political environment of an organisation. This part is concerned with understanding and thriving in complex business environments.

The leaders of your business will try, more or less successfully, to ensure there are consistent and complementary goals and behaviours through strategy and communications. As a manager, even a senior manager, you have a limited ability to shape the environment, but you can respond to it with varying levels of effectiveness.

In a junior role you only need to be aware of part of this environment. You primarily need to understand your direct boss's opinions, needs and limitations. This is discussed in the first two sections of this part. As you become more senior you must develop an understanding of the wider human and political environment of your business. The way you do this is through your network of relationships which is discussed in the third section.

The human and political environment is not just something you must cope with – it is something you can interpret and utilise. Having done this you can create the management role that best fits this environment. This is elaborated in the fourth section.

Deciphering your boss

What is this about and why is it important?

Unless you are a Chief Executive, you are not only a manager, you are also a member of your manager's team. You will probably spend most of your time interacting with your team and this is the focus of this book. But you must also fulfil your role as a member of your manager's team.

Your relationship with your manager or boss is one of the most important relationships at work. Manage it well, and you have a good chance of being successful. Manage it badly, and your success will be at risk.

The foundation of a good relationship is an understanding of your boss's needs and desires. Only if you know these can you fulfil the role your manager wants you to. These needs may be complex and volatile, they may not be written down and nor are they fixed. You have to decipher and monitor your boss to maintain a current understanding of these needs.

Objectives for managers

- To have a clear, comprehensive and up-to-date understanding of your manager's wants and expectations.
- To set realistic expectations with your manager.

Common issues in achieving these objectives

- Bosses provide unclear and incomplete requirements.
- Requirements are mutually contradictory.
- Requirements change frequently.

The management guide

The relationship

There are three main aspects to your relationship with your boss. Your boss is:

1. A source of needs and instructions. I refer to these as your boss's requirements.
2. A resource provider.
3. The person who performs your performance review.

This section focuses on the first of these, but it is important to understand the other two as they are interrelated.

Let's have a closer look at your boss's requirements. These are requirements that you need to understand in order to be able to fulfil her expectations and help her to meet her goals. You can think of these requirements in two categories:

- The formal needs from her role in the business, which cascade down through her onto you and your team.
- Her desires, which are less specific and more related to the person she is, her values, what she wants to achieve and so forth.

The second aspect of your relationship with your boss involves resources. If you have a good relationship with your manager, she will be a resource you can use. She should be someone you can go to for help and advice. On top of this, she is a gateway to other resources. Your manager's power is restricted and resources are limited. But what budget, headcount and other resources are allocated to you depend upon your manager's decisions. These decisions are influenced by how well you interpret and fulfil your manager's requirements.

There are two restrictions on the resources you are allocated: your manager's overall budget and who else it must be shared with. You are in competition with your peers. It is not a zero sum game where any gains for you are always at the expense of your peers. Budgets are flexible and can grow or shrink. But there is a limit, and the more your manager allocates to your peers, the less is available for you.

Your success is not purely about the size of your budget. Sometimes you need few resources, other times you need many. But always you need enough, and ideally a little extra, to deal with the unforeseen (see pp. 173–9). You are most likely to be allocated sufficient resource if you reliably interpret and fulfil your boss's most important needs.

The third aspect of your relationship with your manager is as the person who judges your performance. How your manager assesses your performance depends on a range of factors, but central to her judgement will be your record in meeting her expectations and fulfilling her requirements.

The challenge

Your boss's requirements can be hard to fulfil. This is no surprise, but what may be a surprise is that even understanding these requirements is often difficult. Few managers are certain they are doing the things that have the greatest chance of fulfilling their boss's desires.

Occasionally, you will be lucky and have a boss who is clear about what she wants. Such a boss will be reasonable and will understand the limitations of your team. She will set you achievable and clear objectives. You won't always find yourself in this situation. Bosses' requirements are often ambiguous and imprecise. You have to learn to deal with this. Generally, this challenge increases with seniority. If you want to progress in a management career you must develop the ability to cope with the ambiguity of requirements.

When trying to understand your manager's needs you will encounter the following obstacles:

- Your boss will rarely explain all of her requirements.
- You may interpret your boss's statements and behaviour incorrectly.

- Your boss may have conflicting requirements.
- Your boss's needs will change, sometimes very quickly.
- Even if you understand the requirements, rarely will you have the time or resources to fulfil all of them.

There are many causes of these obstacles. Your boss may assume, incorrectly, that you know her requirements. Your manager has limited time to spend with you. She has a million others things to do, and the time available for you may be too short to explain her requirements. Your boss may not know her own requirements, not having the information from her boss in turn. Like everyone else, your manager is imperfect (see the next section).

Overcoming the challenge

This may seem to make your job impossible. It is not. Every manager has to deal with this challenge, and many people overcome it very well. It is an everyday and resolvable – or at least minimisable – problem.

To understand your manager's requirements you need to be in dialogue with her – regular dialogue. If you only talk to your manager every few months, unless you have an incredibly stable workload, then it is unlikely you will have a deep or current enough understanding of requirements.

Your understanding should not simply be a list of everything your boss wants, you must also seek to understand the context. Which of the requirements are really important, which are nice to have and which are irrelevant? Which requirements must be fulfilled urgently and which ones do you have time to fulfil?

You should seek to have a positive relationship with your manager. A relationship requires interaction, and leads to the opportunity for further interaction. If you have a positive relationship you will get the time to find out the information you need. Also it is far better if you are a colleague that the boss shares and discusses her challenges with, rather than a resource the boss simply dumps work on.

Given the speed with which things change in business, your current understanding of your manager's needs is valid for a limited time. Bosses are not always great at pointing out when needs or priorities have changed. You need to be constantly listening for changes. It is no use effectively fulfilling yesterday's needs.

When your manager explains her requirements make sure you understand them fully. If you do not, probe and ask questions. Be specific in your exploration.

Sometimes you may need a little time to reflect on your understanding. When your manager explains a new requirement, ask for the opportunity to think about how you will fulfil it and for permission to come back later to discuss it. When you come back, show your value by asking specific questions which achieve clarity. By doing this you will often help your manager to improve her own clarity. Normally, she will appreciate this.

If the requirement is complex or different from your usual work, do not simply take it and disappear off to deliver. Your understanding may be flawed, or your manager's explanation may have been incomplete. Think about it and then come back with more questions, and, if possible, examples of what you propose to do. *If I do it like this ... if I give you something that looks like that ... will that fulfil your needs?* If you have clarity and use this to help your manager to achieve greater clarity, then you have already added significant value.

Successful managers help their bosses to develop their understandings of their own requirements, and control their bosses' expectations of how these requirements will be fulfilled.

Often you will not be able to fulfil all of your manager's requirements. This is the time to set expectations. Advise your manager what is and what is not possible, but you should do this in the right way.

Business is an environment which favours positivity, and it is one in which bluntly saying *no*, or *I can't do this*, is frowned upon. When you cannot fulfil a requirement, there are ways of avoiding saying no:

■ **Clarify priorities.** Don't say *I can't do both of these.* Ask *should I do A or B first?*

■ *Define conditions.* Don't say *I can't do this,* say *with x, y and z I can do this.* Even if you know the conditions will never be fulfilled, this is usually better than saying no.

■ **Give choices.** Don't say *I can't do A, B and C.* Say *would you prefer me to do A and B, or A and C?*

In setting expectations you are also trying to avoid taking your manager's problems onto your own back. When you give an unconditional yes to any set of requirements, you have taken the problem completely away from your manager. It is now all yours.

But sometimes you *should* give an unconditional yes to your manager's requirements. Businesses like staff who reliably deliver. This means managing your risks well and not saying yes when you can't do it. But businesses also like managers who say *yes I can do that* without conditions. From time to time you have to take the risk that you will be able to work out requirements and a way of fulfilling them, even if at the time of saying yes you do not know this. Choose the situations carefully, and then manage the risk (see pp. 173–9).

Work on this more if ...

■ You are not confident you understand your boss's requirements.

■ You regularly fail to meet your boss's expectations.

Manager's checklist

■ Your boss is a source of requirements and resources. She also judges your performance.

■ Successful managers interpret their boss's unclear or volatile requirements.

- Seek clarity in your boss's requirements and help your boss to achieve her own clarity.

- Actively set expectations – always try to sound positive.

The imperfect boss

What is this about and why is it important?

If you have read the previous section, and the parts of this book concerned with your relationship with your team (Parts 2 and 4), you may notice a contradiction. I suggest you act in one way with your team, but that you should not expect your boss to act in the same way with you. Why? Because your boss may be imperfect, and you should try to be better than him.

You may be one of the lucky people who has a brilliant line manager. Most people come across brilliant managers at some point in their careers. But there are many imperfect bosses. At times you will work for one. In this situation, your job is not to equal him, but to be better. Sometimes this means carefully picking what you learn from your boss. In other situations, you become a good manager in spite of your boss's quirks.

The likelihood of having a flawed boss at some time is high. One of my career disappointments was finding out that the percentage of people who are useless at their job stays about the same irrespective of seniority. You may expect the most senior people to be highly talented individuals you can learn from. Some of them will be, but if 25% of your colleagues are not up to scratch at your current level, you will find 25% are not up to scratch at the next level, and the one above that – all the way to the top.

There are lots of reasons for poor managers. Sometimes an individual was lucky in getting a promotion they did not deserve. This person may be smart, but as I discussed at the start of Part 2, smartness does not equate to great management. Sometimes your boss was a high performer in his previous job and was promoted based on this performance. Unfortunately, his skills in the previous role are not the ones required in his present role. (This has been eloquently generalised in *The Peter Principle*: 'in a *hierarchy every employee tends to rise to their level of incompetence'*, Laurence J. Peter and Raymond Hull; Souvenir Press, 1969.) Also there is a limited pool of talented people around. Often the person in a job is not the ideal candidate, but the least bad choice. Your boss may be one of these.

You have to learn to work with imperfect bosses. One of the upsides is that the limited number of brilliant managers means if you become a great manager, the chances are you will shine.

Objectives for managers

- To be able to cope with and perform your management role with an imperfect boss.
- To understand what to learn from your boss and what to ignore.

Common issues in achieving these objectives

- Lack of experience leads you to judge bad management as the norm.
- Viewing bad management as unavoidable.

The management guide

There are many ways of being a poor manager. Poor managers may be uncaring, uncommunicative, self-serving, unreasonable, or simply incompetent. Over time these people mostly get caught out, but not always. But your career cannot wait for your boss's limitations to become apparent to other people.

Alternatively, you may have a competent boss, but he still may manage you poorly. Perhaps his attention is elsewhere or he is biased against you for some reason. Maybe he did not choose you and as a result feels encumbered with someone he does not want.

In either case, what should you do? There are four steps to handling this situation:

1. Have realistic expectations. Do you have a poor boss or unrealistic expectations?
2. Use the existing business mechanisms to make sure your boss knows he is a poor manager.
3. Decide if you are going to take formal action and complain.
4. Assuming you are not taking formal action, deal with the imperfect manager.

Reasonable and unreasonable expectations

Always remember your boss is human. All those uncertainties that you feel, he probably does as well. All those limits in information he gives you, he may suffer from too. You are not perfect, nobody else you have ever met is perfect – why should your boss be?

Differentiate behaviour that is unreasonable from behaviour you do not like or that does not meet your expectations. The business you work in should value you and treat you fairly. But fairly is not always the same as how you want to be treated. Your role exists because the business needs an outcome achieved. It does not exist to make you happy.

If you are unsure whether you have a bad boss or not, ask friends or peers about their bosses. If your boss is behaving similarly to theirs, it is probably your expectations that are unrealistic. On the other hand, if your boss is significantly worse, then he may be unreasonable or incompetent.

One reason for dissatisfaction is the support a manager provides to you. The amount of support you should expect depends on seniority. If you have a senior role then support will be limited – you should be able to swim by yourself. You may be given high-level objectives – beyond that you have to work it out for yourself. But as a junior manager or team leader you should have regular coaching and help from your manager. You should not only be told what to do, but should also get advice on how to do it.

Feeding back

Ideally, if you have a bad manager he should know he is a bad manager. But feedback does not always work. It takes a very confident individual to tell an egotistical and volatile boss that he is a poor manager. It is naive to think it is risk-free to tell your manager he is not very good. However, if you can, you should find ways of doing this.

Helpfully, in many organisations there are mechanisms to do this, such as 360-degree feedback. If these exist use them. Try to be as specific as possible in providing feedback – and link it to desired outcomes. What specifically does your boss do or not do which gets in the way of your doing your job?

If you have a relationship in which your boss asks you for feedback, or in which you feel you can tell him, then do. But be careful how you feed back to someone more senior. Rather than saying someone is not good, phrase it positively and link the feedback to the potential for better outcomes. Tell him something like: *if you interacted with me in this way ... I could do more of ...* or *if you did this ... I could improve performance by ...*

Making a complaint

One answer to the poor boss is to make a formal complaint. You can complain to HR or to a more senior manager. This is a big decision to make, and you should not complain about your boss lightly. If you complain, and your complaint is not upheld, it can make the relationship much worse.

However, there are valid reasons to complain and to complain quickly. Do complain if your boss:

- Is bullying you.
- Exhibits unacceptable biases, e.g. racism, sexism, ageism, disability bias.
- Is encouraging you to engage in illegal or seriously unethical behaviour.

Make sure you are clear what the complaint is. Have evidence to back it up and expect your complaint to be challenged. One person's bullying is another's high-energy team-building. One person's unethical behaviour is another's flexible interpretation of guidelines in that context.

Fortunately, these situations are rare. In most circumstances you do not need to complain about the imperfect boss. You just deal with him.

Dealing with the imperfect manager

If you have a bad boss, and assuming you are not going to simply ignore him, there are two things you can do. You can work with him, perhaps helping him to become a better manager, or you can work around him. Of course, you can do both.

Learn from your boss. Even the worst boss provides lessons to learn from – even if they are what not to do. If you have the inclination and ability to do it, try to build a strong relationship with your boss. With a deep relationship you may, sensitively, be able to give him the feedback everyone else struggles with. Alternatively, you can help him to do the tasks he performs poorly. No manager is good at everything and he may value your ability to do some of the things he is weaker at.

The alternative is to work around your boss. Your manager is not the only person with influence, power or resources. He is not the only person you can learn from, or who will help your career progress. You should seek to build a wider network than your boss alone (see the next section). As you build your network make yourself and your achievements visible to senior stake-holders. I have met successful managers who have nothing to do with their line managers, relying purely on other stakeholders. Generally, I do not advise going to that extreme, but neither would I rely on a single line manager.

One thing to avoid is politicking or bad-mouthing your boss at work. Unless you are a sophisticated politician with a network of powerful supporters the chances are it will backfire onto you. A bad boss who thinks you have been manoeuvring around him is a dangerous combination.

There are situations in which you cannot help your boss or work your way around him. This is the time to make a decision to move on. You don't need to do it immediately, but life is too short and too valuable to work for bad bosses for too long. You will only be miserable and learn bad habits.

A final piece of advice concerning terrible bosses. The worst bosses have a reputation for being bad. If you know their reputation, avoid them in the first place. When you choose and accept a role, consider who will be your manager. Choose bosses who will help in your career or who you can learn from. If he has nothing to teach you and cannot help your career, do not work for him.

Work on this more if ...

■ You are concerned about your manager's behaviour or are becoming frustrated working for him.

Manager's checklist

■ Imperfect managers are a fact of life in business.

■ If you have a poor manager work with him and try to improve his performance, and work around him by building a network of alternative sponsors and supporters.

■ If nothing else works – move on. Take care choosing whom you work for in future.

Think networks, not hierarchies

What is this about and why is it important?

Most organisation charts and recruitment processes reinforce the concept of *a* boss. But your boss is just one stakeholder amongst many. You will be involved in numerous activities that lie outside of your boss's domain. There are project teams and task forces, cross-process and matrix reporting lines, and all sorts of other associations of allegiances and common interests. You are part of a network, not simply a hierarchy.

It would be wrong to think your boss does not matter. He or she does and will continue to do so. The relationship with your boss is usually the most important relationship you have. But it is not so important that you can ignore everyone else. There are many other stakeholders who can allocate or influence the allocation of work to you and your team, who can provide access to resources and who are involved in judging your performance. There are many people who can help you be a success or get in the way of your success. Sometimes it will not feel as if you have one boss, but several.

Thinking only of the hierarchy is the wrong way to focus. Businesses exist to satisfy customers by creating something of value for them. Value is not created and customers are not satisfied because work passes up and down functional hierarchies. Value is derived and customer needs are fulfilled by the end-to-end execution of processes which cut across functions and departments. Processes and process optimisation are more important than hierarchy and functional excellence.

You have distinct, but often overlapping, professional and social networks. This section is only concerned with your professional network. I use the word *relationship* as shorthand for *professional relationship*.

Objectives for managers

■ To identify the individuals you want to have professional relationships with.

■ To build a strong, productive web of professional relationships.

Common issues in achieving these objectives

■ Too great a focus on the hierarchy.

■ Ad hoc relationship building leading to a sub-optimal network.

■ Lack of knowledge of how to build a network.

The management guide

The network of relationships you develop will enable you to gain influence and power. Relationships, influence and power allow you to get things done. But there is no map of the best relationships to have. To build a powerful network, you have to create your own map.

The professional relationships you build depend on two factors: luck and the actions you take to develop relationships. You will not have the time to develop meaningful relationships with everyone. There may be relationships which are not obviously beneficial, which later turn out to be helpful. However, it is worth focusing on those that are most likely to be helpful. A good network requires exploration and choices. Pick the relationships you build.

Building a complex web of stakeholders creates problems as well as benefits. Successful teams have common, shared, clear goals. The simpler these goals are, the easier it is to keep everyone aligned. Different stakeholders have different goals and desires. As you build relationships you may need to help various stakeholders achieve their desires and goals. A common business strategy creates a level of consistency between different stakeholder goals, but is not the complete answer. Having a complex set of stakeholders challenges your ability to have clear and simple goals. The network makes your life complex with varying objectives, subjective views and ambiguous options.

As a junior manager you have a choice to develop a wide network or not. You can choose to keep your head down working for your boss. But this will limit your potential and will constrain you and your team's ability to do exceptional work. As a senior manager you have little choice but to build a network. It is the way organisations work.

Valuable relationships

A network of worthwhile relationships is not just knowing lots of people. Any of the people you know may turn out to be helpful and useful to you, and you cannot always predict which relationships will be most useful. But there are relationships which are more likely to be valuable. Individuals you can turn to for help, advice, resources or information. Generally, more relationships are better than fewer, but deeper relationships are better than more.

Relationships are bilateral. They are built not just because you choose to build them, but also because the other party chooses to build one with you. It's not just what you can gain from having a relationship, it is what the other party gains by having a relationship with you. Therefore before you start to build your network think about what makes you an attractive person for others to network with.

Whom should you choose to build relationships with? You only have a limited amount of time, and you cannot build valuable relationships with everyone. You need to decide whom to invest in building relationships with. Seek professional relationships where:

- You gain help, advice and useful information.
- You gain direct access to influence.
- You gain indirect access to influence, via the professional relationships of people you have relationships with.

■ You become visible to people you want to be visible to.

■ You gain access to skills or other resources.

The people who can fulfil the needs described in the points above are a varied bunch. It may seem obvious, but it is worth stating – relationships are with individuals, not with teams or departments. The individuals include your peers and senior managers. However, some influential people are relatively junior, having specialist expertise or relationships with groups like trade unions. Do not limit yourself to internal relationships. Many good mentors are external to your organisation. A satisfied customer, who is willing to express their satisfaction to important people in your organisation, can be more helpful than a supportive internal stakeholder.

The management hierarchy is part of your network. If you can, develop a strong relationship with your boss and their boss too. But do not get fixated on the line hierarchy. Lots of things work across the business, and you will miss these if you focus purely on hierarchy.

We tend to be attracted to people who are similar to ourselves. If you examine most people's networks they are full of people with common interests. Perhaps you need some common interest to develop a relationship. But try to develop a varied network. Diverse people who are dissimilar to you will be helpful, bringing different experiences, information, views, contacts and access to varied resources.

Building your network

You will naturally develop relationships with a range of people as part of your daily work. Take advantage of chance meetings with people, but do not rely on this. People with powerful networks deliberately build them. They identify the people who are advantageous to have a relationship with and go out of their way to meet them.

Sometimes to develop a strong relationship you have to put in more than you can get out initially. If you are going to meet someone for the first time whom you want to develop a relationship with, plan the meeting. What can you say, indicate or offer that will make them want to develop a relationship with you? It is always good to have a short 'elevator pitch' with which you can quickly explain your role and what makes you and your team special in a few sentences.

When you join a new organisation you need to put particular effort into building your network. But maintaining a network is a never-ending task. A network is dynamic and ever-changing. It needs constant maintenance and enhancement. New people join organisations, roles change, power shifts. You need to be monitoring this and tailoring your network accordingly. It is sometimes said that as a manager you manage at two levels, with individuals in your team, and with the team as a whole. I believe you can add a third level to this: your network.

Your political skills will be useful in building, maintaining and utilising your network. The word *politics* is often seen as a dirty phrase in business. But political skills are not bad in themselves. They can be applied to bad ends, but they are essential skills. Wherever there are people, there is politics. You cannot avoid it – and you must be able to deal with it. Politics is not your enemy. It is a tool to be used. Without it, you will not get far.

Use your extended network, no matter how small, to increase the number of your relationships. Ask people you trust who should you develop relationships with? If they know people whom you would benefit by knowing, ask for an introduction. Return the favour. Individuals who get introduced to useful people are usually the ones who also help others to build their networks.

Using your network

A network is only of value if it is useful. Use your network to:

- Understand the organisation, and use this information in creating your role (see next section).
- Keep track of what is going on. There is lots of useful information that is never disseminated in formal briefings.

■ Make yourself and your team visible. This helps with being involved in the most interesting work and also with promotions.

■ Gain access to the scarce resources that will assist in fulfilling your objectives.

■ Provide help to others who value your assistance.

One of the dangers of a large network is that you are constantly asked for help or to be involved in activities. You will also be swamped with more information than you can cope with. Therefore two of the key skills for a good networker are: learning to say no, without appearing unhelpful, and the ability to filter information and only process what is relevant.

Work on this more if ...

■ You do not understand the value of a good network.

■ Your network is not sufficiently useful to you.

■ You regularly feel you would be more successful if you had relationships with other people in the organisation.

Manager's checklist

■ A network, extending beyond the normal management hierarchy, is essential.

■ Good networks do not happen by chance – they are consciously planned and built.

■ Relationships are bilateral – you cannot only take from a network, you must give to it.

■ A professional network is only of value if it is useful.

Creating your role

What is this about and why is it important?

Part 1 looked at the types of activity that make up a manager's job. Parts 2 and 3 explored the various people with stakes in your role: yourself, your team, your boss and the management hierarchy, and a host of other stakeholders. In this section all these elements are brought together to investigate how you create your management role.

There are givens in any management position, things you must or must not do. You work within a specific environment with a certain culture and expectations. There are documented descriptions of your role, such as job specifications, competency frameworks and performance objectives. You must understand these, but at best they add up to an incomplete picture. You have to search out the full requirements and create your own role.

Objectives for managers

- To develop the fullest possible understanding of your role.
- To maintain this understanding as the situation evolves.
- To select the optimal activities to perform.

Common issues in achieving these objectives

- Incomplete, volatile information, much of which is ambiguous.
- Limited guidance.

The management guide

Context: the spectrum of roles

There is a spectrum in business roles. At one end of this spectrum are fully defined roles with limited discretion. At the other end are roles with limited definition and almost total discretion.

The most junior roles in organisations tend to be typified by high levels of definition and limited discretion. There is a set of tasks to be done, an order to do them in, and a procedure to follow. The organisation strives to make the performance of these roles ever more efficient, applying standardisation and best practice, utilising tools like Six Sigma and Lean. Performance is tightly measured, and the measurement intervals are short; sometimes measurement is continuous. Not all organisations have roles like this: professional services firms, for instance, do not. But many do: for example, the staff in a call centre.

With seniority discretion tends to increase. There may still be a defined role, but how things are done is more open to the holder's choice. A person holding the role utilises expertise and experience to make judgements.

As seniority increases, the level of role definition decreases further. More aspects of the role are decided by the role holder. At the highest level perhaps only annual objectives are defined, and even these are negotiated. Once targets are set, what and how they are done is completely up to the role holder. The role holder constantly monitors the situation, makes choices and judgements, takes action and dynamically alters priorities and focus.

As a manager you sit some way along this spectrum. You may have a reasonably well-defined role but you will also be expected to exercise discretion and judgement. With a career in management you will continually move away from defined roles towards roles in which you have more and more discretion.

The features of discretionary roles

Discretionary roles involve:

- The need to make choices about what to do and how to do it, but limited information on the options.
- Many stakeholders with differing needs. It is naive to assume that interests will be aligned – at times there will be contradiction between the needs of stakeholders.
- Volatile needs. What is critical in a business one day tends not to be next.
- Constrained resources and time. Even where interests are aligned, you will not have the time or resource to fulfil them all.

When you take your first management job no one will tell you *all* the things that can be considered as part of your role, what must be focused on and what should be ignored, what the priorities are and so on. You will only be told some of them. Other things will become apparent in dribs and drabs, constantly change, or remain unclear. Somehow, you have to make sense of this situation.

Some people respond to this by panic and confusion. Individuals newly promoted to management roles sometimes find the level of ambiguity overwhelming. But after a while most people get used to it.

Your management role is not defined for you. You must explore it and then create it. It is *your* management role.

Exploring, creating and thriving

What is your role? Given all the variables it may be impossible to give the perfect answer to this question. But there are answers which are wrong, satisfactory, good or better. You obviously want to avoid the wrong answers. Whether you want to find the satisfactory, good or better answer is up to you and your ambition.

Although you do not have total freedom it is up to you to shape the role. Start by:

- *Identifying givens*: the unquestionable things you must do and how must you do them.

- *Limiting the role*: you will not please everyone. Identify anyone you must please and those you can overlook. If you are unsure to start with, begin with your boss.
- *Ignoring what you cannot influence* (see pp. 180–4).
- *Taking advice*: find a guide to help you through this. This may be your boss, a senior peer or some other mentor. Many people are willing to be of help if asked.

Identify the givens by observing people's behaviour. You want to find the real essentials, not just the things people say must be done. This is best explained by a couple of examples:

- Many organisations have apparently mandatory administrative processes, but in some businesses you will find many people whose careers have never been harmed by ignoring these processes. In this situation, these processes are not mandatory.
- In some organisations you may have to submit regular budget updates. If you find that everyone scurries around like crazy to do these, dropping any other work – this is mandatory.

You cannot learn the real givens from a management book. You learn them by observing and listening to your business and its culture.

There are other things you can do that will help you understand and become at ease with your role:

- *Accept you cannot do everything*: no manager does, nor should you try to either.
- *Start unadventurously*: do the things which your closest stakeholders (usually your boss and your peers in his team) do and want done.
- *Limit your risk*: seek approval for what you are doing and manage expectations. Tell your boss what you intend to do, what you will not be doing. Confirm this is what he wants.
- *Avoid big promises*: there will come a time to make big promises. Your first few days in a management role are not the time to do this.

One of the golden rules is that you must keep doing something. Managers cannot disappear off into a quiet room for days and days to analyse the situation. Your boss expects you to do things. Your team needs you to give guidance, define priorities, and make decisions. This cannot wait. It is generally better to be doing sub-optimal management activities than to be doing nothing at all. You will also learn more by performing the management role than by thinking about it.

As you become more familiar with your role and your network grows, become more adventurous and experiment. Take small steps, by doing different things. Find what actions get praise and reward, and do more of them. Find what actions get censure or penalty, and avoid them. Identify which actions give you what you want – find a way of doing these. Once you are confident you can take some risks (see pp. 173–9).

You are not alone, and do not have to find everything out by yourself. Observe those around you, especially those who are successful, and work out what they do that your less successful peers do not. Listen to your experienced peers' conversations. Then create your role.

Do not stop shaping your role. When you become a new manager making sense of the situation is one of the biggest and hardest tasks. It is a task that never goes away as businesses continue to change and adapt. So must you. You will find after a while that this making sense out of the unclear becomes second nature and even subconscious, and then you will really thrive as a manager.

Work on this more if ...

- You do not understand your role, are confused or feel lost.
- You regularly find out there are aspects to the job you have not performed but you were expected to.

Manager's checklist

■ Do not expect the full definition of your role to be given on a plate.

■ What definition is given will be incomplete.

■ Observe, listen and make sense of your role. Continue to make sense.

■ If you are unsure, start with a limited, unadventurous role and expand as your confidence and experience grow.

■ But whatever state you are in, keep doing something.

four

The working team

In Parts 1–3 we explored understanding your role and building your team. Once you understand your role and have a team, you are in a position to engage the team in work. This is the topic of Part 4.

To work effectively your team needs two fundamental types of guidance from you: a shared sense of direction and the definition of the tasks to be done by the team. How this is done is described in the first two sections.

Work rarely goes perfectly smoothly, and as a manager you will have to make various management interventions to maintain direction and help team members overcome problems. The third section compares two ways of performing these interventions: as a directive manager and as a coach.

Finally, the fourth section describes how your team works with the wider set of resources available in the organisation.

Marching to the same tune

What is this about and why is it important?

The rationale to form teams is that they accomplish more than people would individually. Teams succeed when the team members' work is consistent and pulling in the same direction, in other words when team members have shared goals. Teams fail when goals are unclear, not shared or not accepted.

The standard tool for ensuring shared goals in business is *strategy*. A strategy is developed and shared with staff. The strategy aims to align behaviour towards common goals. Business success depends on the right strategy and the alignment of activity in the organisation with the strategy.

An individual team does not need a strategy. But there is a need for a shared sense of direction which team members are aligned in working towards. I call this sense of direction a *vision*. For your team it is *your* vision.

Team members expect their managers to provide a vision. A new manager with a new team is looked to, impatiently, to share a vision quickly. The vision enables the team to understand the context for their work and the direction they should be going in. It is the vision, as much as detailed task instructions, that enables the team's individuals to march to the same tune.

People respond well to a clear sense of direction. A lack of direction is demotivating for many. Hence those moans of the form: *we have no vision,* or *we don't know what we're up to,* and *if only there was a decent strategy.*

There is a trend for organisations to encourage more empowered, autonomous, self-directing sub-groups and individuals. Such sub-groups and individuals select and prioritise tasks, and decide how to do them, without constant recourse to their manager. Some of this trend is lip service to the concept of empowered staff. The words are used but no real empowerment is offered. Where empowerment is real, there is an increased need for a shared vision. Without a manager instructing staff and constantly monitoring their steps, if no shared vision is referred to by team members, alignment will disappear. The best that will happen is inefficiency. Chaos is more likely.

Objectives for managers

■ A clear direction for the team, aligned with your goals.

■ For team members to adopt this direction.

■ An efficient team working towards common goals.

Common issues in achieving these objectives

■ Too much focus on the day-to-day details, with no time left to think where it leads.

■ Inability to synthesise complexity into a single simple vision.

■ Lack of understanding of wider context, leading to poor visions.

■ Insufficient effort spent communicating and reinforcing the vision.

The management guide

Vision matters and should be seen to matter. A vision requires effort to create, maintain, share and convince team members to follow. An effective vision, which your team embraces and works towards, will give you a productive team. A poor vision is at best a waste of time and at worst destructive. It is important to get it right.

A vision encapsulates why the team exists, what it does, where it is going and why it should go there. Like a good advert, given the context and history of the team, a vision may imply far more than the words actually say. There is no one right vision. But an effective vision has certain characteristics. Visions can take a variety of forms. Examples of visions are:

■ To provide an excellent order processing service continuously reducing customer delivery timescales.

■ To supply graphic design services at a lower price than but an equal quality to any external provider.

■ To be *the* project managers of choice within the business.

Effective visions

An effective vision is easy to communicate. A vision does not need to be grand or complex. In fact complexity is best avoided. The purpose of a vision is to give all team members something they can refer to continuously, thinking *does what I am doing contribute towards this vision? If so, do more of it. If not, cease.* A simple image described in one (or a few) sentences achieves this best.

A good vision is meaningful to the team, relates to its work and is in words your team members are comfortable with. You are not trying to get the team to follow your instructions, but to accept and embrace a vision which they feel part of.

A productive vision is perceived as possible, but also it should be stretching. A good vision is measurable. You can assess progress against the vision, and your team can assess their own progress. Seeing progress against goals provides excellent positive reinforcement and motivation for individuals to develop and repeat the behaviour(s) you want.

Ideally, the vision is compatible with team members' beliefs and expectations. It should be the sort of picture of the world that people intuitively feel is right, even if it is the first time they have seen or heard it. This cannot always be achieved. Sometimes team members' beliefs and expectations need to change. If the vision is contrary to current beliefs or expectations then you must expect to exert more effort explaining it and getting it accepted.

The vision for a team does not need to be innovative or unique. Your vision is not a competitive strategy in the open market, it is a compass for the team.

A vision gives your team a context and a basis to make judgements and choices. The greater the level of discretion amongst team members is, the clearer the vision needs to be. If you want your team members to be more self-directed, stop providing them with detailed work instructions and give them a direction and a goal. Let them work out the details.

Influences on your vision

The business environment is complex. One of your jobs is to understand this complexity and to work out a route through it. Acting as a sense maker who clarifies the different requirements for your team is one of the most valuable things you can do. Once you have a sense of direction you have the basis for your vision, and this can be communicated back to your team.

Your vision is developed from your interpretation of a number of ideas, desires and information. It is not an exercise in imaginative thinking. The main sources for your vision are:

- The external requirements on the team: from the management hierarchy and other stakeholders.
- Your personal view about how the team should progress and develop.
- The perspectives of members of the team, should you choose to listen to them.

The primary source for your vision is often the company strategy, mission and vision statements. If these are clear and meaningful for your team you may just be able to use them directly. If they are not, they may need to be translated for your team. Do not be worried if your vision seems obvious to you – this is a good sign, not a sign of a lack of thinking. The role of most teams in the organisation is straightforward.

Ideally the vision is built from the perspectives and opinions of your team members. Your team should live and work to the vision. This is far easier to achieve if team members are involved in defining what the vision of the team is.

Using the vision

A vision will not become shared with the team unless you communicate it regularly and clearly. Repetition is critical. If you want to communicate it successfully, the vision must be simple. This is not to patronise or underestimate your team's intellectual capabilities, but because only clear and simple directions are remembered and constantly referred to.

Communications need to be tailored to the audience and the context. Different team members need different types of information communicated in different ways. As manager you have to develop an understanding of your team members' communication preferences. Some team members only need to know why the vision is being pursued – they are capable and prefer to fill in the gaps. Other team members will want more information. For some a vision will start to feel less like giving a sense of direction and more like providing precise instructions (see pp. 95–100).

It is not just what you say in communicating your vision, but how it is said as well that will affect how successful your communications are. You can shape people's interpretation and attitude towards a vision by framing it in the right way. Focus on the positive features of a vision and the positive outcomes from achieving it.

More important to the acceptance of your vision than communications is your behaviour. Your team will follow what you do – not what you say. The honesty of your vision soon becomes apparent in your behaviour. No one will believe a vision unless you live it, and make decisions that are aligned with it – and critically only reward performance and behaviour that are consistent with it. If you frequently act contrary to the vision, including making decisions which go against it or rewarding behaviour which is divergent with it, you may be followed as the manager, but the vision will not be.

Visions and the real world

There will always be activities to be undertaken that do not fit the vision. At certain times of year, for example annual budget planning, you may find more work than usual which is not contributing towards achieving your vision. This is unavoidable. Work does not always fit into well-structured compartments and boundaries. However, work that does not fit the vision should be the exception and not the norm. If the majority of your work is not aligned with the vision, you have the wrong vision or you are selecting and prioritising the wrong activities.

A vision will not be achieved at once. You must manage your own and team member expectations that worthwhile visions take a while to accomplish.

Work on this more if ...

■ You do not have a clear sense of direction for the team.

■ Team members regularly complain that they do not understand the strategy or the purpose of the team.

■ You are unable to delegate work to team members without maintaining excessive oversight.

Manager's checklist

■ A key role for a manager is making sense of the business environment, and determining a clear, simple, meaningful direction for the team.

■ A shared sense of direction and common goals are essential for effective teams and empowerment of individuals.

■ The most successful visions are built with the involvement and ideas of your team members.

■ Communicating vision is a significant and ongoing task for a manager.

■ Your team will watch what you do more than listen to what you say. Your behaviour must be consistent with the vision.

Cutting up the cake

What is this about and why is it important?

It is obvious that you cannot personally do all the team's work. It has to be shared out amongst team members. What you delegate, whom work is allocated to and how you distribute it are some of the most fundamental choices you make.

There are various, conflicting goals in delegating. How you delegate affects the productivity and motivation of the team. Over time, the choices you make in allocating work also affect risk and the value of the team to the business.

Delegation is a continuous, everyday task for managers. Delegation decisions can be complex, but they are frequent and cannot become onerous. You need to develop the skills to assess situations rapidly and find the right balance between delegation outcomes.

As a manager, you are measured by team results. Your personal performance or the performance of any individual in the team only matters in so far as it contributes to the team result. This team result is the responsibility of one person – you. If a team member struggles or is not performing that is an issue for you to deal with. Everyone struggling indicates bad management. The root cause is often a history of poor delegation, but delegation is within your control.

Objectives for managers

- To balance individuals' desires with team needs in terms of work allocation.
- To balance immediate productivity requirements with longer-term skills development and risk management.
- To support team member motivation and engagement.

Common issues in achieving these objectives

■ Everyday pressures and productivity targets encourage short-term focus.

■ Unwillingness of managers to let go of activity.

■ Risk avoidance leading to overly cautious task allocation.

The management guide

The balancing act

Good delegation balances contending needs.

Primarily, you delegate to find efficient and effective ways to complete the team's work. You want a productive team that can process as much work as possible to the appropriate standard. But you also want to motivate the team. Different team members aspire to do different work. How you allocate work directly impacts team member engagement.

The situation becomes more complex when you consider longer-term perspectives. The way you allocate work across the team affects individuals' progress and the skills they develop. You can allocate work to individuals based on current skills, building a team with individuals with deep specific expertise. Alternatively, you can share the work across the team so everyone does some of everything, developing a team with common shared skills. Deep expertise has benefits, but it also increases risk.

The narrower the specialisation and the fewer common skills across the team, the more you are exposed to problems if a team member is absent or leaves. In some specialist areas, having a few staff with specialist skills poses a significant risk for a business. Such individuals may be junior, but if they perform a vital role that no one else can do, you have heightened risk. On the other hand, allocating work evenly across the team so everyone develops common skills is not always productive.

These conflicting pressures can be summarised as follows:

- For productivity you allocate people work that they know and have done countless times before. For motivation and interest you allow individuals to do novel and different activities.

- For maximum productivity you allocate work to the most capable members of the team. For learning and development you allocate work to less capable members of the team.

- From the individual perspective you want each team member to be motivated, enjoying their work and learning. From a team's perspective you need to maximise short- and long-term productivity and minimise business risk. These are related, but not identical goals.

Achieving the right outcomes is a dynamic balancing act. At some times productivity is paramount, at others you can delegate work for motivation and learning reasons. It is an equilibrium you need to be aware of, constantly seeking to achieve the best balance.

How you delegate

Once you have decided whom you are going to allocate work to, the next issue is how you instruct individuals. There is a spectrum going from giving a detailed definition of how you want a task performed through to only indicating the goal required, leaving the individual to work out the details of how to do it.

What instructions you give depends on the individual and the situation. Generally, more experienced individuals need less guidance. If you want people to develop you need to reduce the amount of information you provide and encourage individuals to work out details for themselves. However, in high-pressure situations with tight deadlines or critical activities, there is a natural tendency to minimise risk by being prescriptive and cautious in whom you allocate work to.

There are benefits in taking risk. For many people it is motivational to be trusted to do demanding tasks without detailed instructions. Additionally, team members will learn most when allocated the demanding tasks. For the team to develop you must take some risks. You can balance this by monitoring progress (see pp. 116–23).

You should coach your team members to become effective at exploring, understanding and accepting work. To do this they need to learn to ask the right questions before accepting work. You can assist them in developing these skills by encouraging them to plan their own work rather than your providing it fully defined.

You do not want to be involved in allocating every task, or you will be swamped. You want to set up a system where it is obvious how work should be allocated, with team members self-allocating tasks. If you achieve this, your role involves less allocating tasks and more ensuring the right balance between productivity, learning and motivation.

Your management workload

It may seem obvious what tasks are to be delegated to team members. In reality, it is not always clear cut. There is work for the team and there are management tasks for you. The boundary between the two is blurred. Even management tasks can be delegated. Your job is to ensure the tasks are done, not necessarily to do them yourself.

Examples of work you can delegate across the team are as varied as budget planning, chairing meetings, coaching junior team members, giving presentations or representing the team at events.

How much of the management workload can you allocate to the team? You must consider factors like the skills of the team, the capacity to take on management tasks, the sensitivity and appropriateness of some of the work and so on. But it also depends on your desires and how important it is for team members to develop management skills.

You create value by developing management skills in your team, and make it easier for yourself to be promoted. If you never allocate management tasks to team members they will never learn how to become managers. If you are indispensable, you cannot be promoted. If there is someone who can take over from you, then you can be promoted.

Your role is justified by the performance of the team, not by how busy you are personally. Avoid holding on to all the management tasks because you feel you need to be busy to justify your role. As well as adding value to the business, you can make your own life easier by delegating some of your management workload.

Do you want to work masses of overtime or go home at a sensible time in the evening? You have significant discretion over how much you personally do versus how much you ensure is done by other team members. There is a balance to be found as a team will not respond well to a manager who is perceived as workshy, and your boss will not praise you if she regularly sees you doing nothing.

Ask yourself for any task you do: can someone else in the team do this, will anyone else in the team benefit by doing it? How much of your work do you need to do and how much do you choose to do? Usually, you can trust people more than you expect, and even if it goes wrong the world does not collapse and there will be valuable lessons to learn.

Three myths

I want to finish this section by looking at three misleading assumptions many managers make. The trio of myths are:

- Multitasking is good.
- The best team is the busiest team.
- A team can be flexible and fully utilised.

The first assumption is that multitasking is something to aspire to. Multitasking is often essential, and it is a real talent to be able to do it well. That does not mean that it should be aspired to. Multitasking is usually more inefficient than starting and completing one task at a time. The real world is messy. Activities arise which are urgent and must be done now. Some tasks have natural breaks when you must wait for other actions to happen. These facts make multitasking a necessity. But you should only multitask when you need to. It should not be done out of choice.

There is also an assumption that the best team is a busy team. The most value-adding team in business is the one that completes the most value-adding tasks. The aim is to be productive, not to be busy. Often you will be busy – but being busy is a fact and not a goal. Adding value without being busy is true efficiency.

The third myth is that a manager must keep their team fully utilised whilst having sufficient resource to respond to peaks in workload. You cannot do both. You can be flexible by having a level of excess resource – or by keeping people busy on tasks that can be dropped at a moment's notice. Alternatively, you can be 100% utilised on important high-priority work. You have to decide whether flexibility or high utilisation is more important.

Work on this more if ...

- Your team is unproductive or inflexible, or not developing necessary skills.
- You are dependent on a few skilled individuals in key areas.
- Team members are bored or lack interest in their work.
- You have no obvious successor.

Manager's checklist

- Delegation is a fundamental everyday task for all managers.
- How you delegate impacts productivity, motivation, skills development and risk.
- You can delegate much of your management workload. Doing so increases skills and your freedom to be promoted.
- Multitasking and being busy are necessary evils, not goals in themselves.

Coach or controller?

What is this about and why is it important?

There will be many situations in which you need to support the work of your staff. Problems will arise, barriers will occur which team members cannot see their way around, instructions will be misinterpreted, progress will be too slow, and the quality of work will not be as required. In each of these cases there will be a need for a management intervention.

There will also be, from time to time, interpersonal issues between members of the team. Often it is best if you do not get involved in these, leaving them to team members to resolve. But on occasions professional relationships can break down to such an extent that they damage team performance or team cohesion. Then you must intervene.

There are different ways of intervening to resolve these types of problem. A helpful way is to consider two extremes. At one extreme you act as a coach; at the other you are a controlling manager who gives direction and instructions.

- *As a controlling manager*: you determine the solution to problems and the appropriate actions. You direct the individual on the steps to take.
- *As a coach*: you encourage individuals to uncover their innate knowledge to resolve issues. This is done by asking questions which encourage the individual's thinking. They personally identify solutions and appropriate actions.

There are advantages and disadvantages to each approach. If you are an expert in the problem area, being directive quickly comes to a solution which matches your perspective on what is right. Coaching can take more time, but often results in a more sustainable result. Individuals learn how to resolve issues of this nature for themselves and need less help in future.

Understanding when to be a controlling manager and when to be a coach will make you a more effective manager.

Objectives for managers

- To develop both controlling/directive and coaching styles of management interventions.
- To use the most appropriate type of intervention for the situation.

Common issues in achieving these objectives

- Lack of awareness, ability or willingness to use coaching skills.
- Some business culture does not favour coaching.
- Unwillingness of some team members to respond to coaching.

The management guide

Understanding the difference between coaching and being directive requires some explanation. Imagine you observe a team member struggling with a problem, and you realise that you are going to have to intervene to help. There are two considerations:

- Who initiates the intervention?
- What is the nature of the intervention?

There is no black and white rule. But typically a directive manager will initiate interventions with staff. The intervention will usually be in the form of an instruction, telling the individual what to do. Help is pushed onto team members. A coach is more likely to leave a team member to decide when they need help. When assistance is sought, it is more likely to be in the form of exploratory questions, which are designed to help individuals work out a solution to their problem themselves. Individuals use the coach to pull help from themselves.

Which approach is best? That depends on what you are trying to achieve in intervening in the specific situation at hand. If your sole aim is to ensure a task is completed rapidly, to a high level of quality and precisely as you desire – take a directive approach. If you are trying to help the individual to grow, to understand their work more profoundly and to use their own creativity – utilise a coaching style.

Underlying this is your mental model of your role as a manager (see pp. 19–23). Do you see yourself as someone who is hands-on controlling the team and what they do, or do you see yourself in a more facilitative role enabling team members to do the tasks they need to get done?

Coaching

Coaching can be an unfamiliar or uncomfortable style of inter-action for some managers. But once you have got used to it, you will find it empowering for both your team and yourself.

There are significant advantages to coaching team members. In a coaching relationship the team member takes full responsibility for their work, and for their personal development. The development of team members is the key advantage of coaching. It has been shown time and time again that people who are always told what to do learn less than individuals who are encouraged to develop their own understanding. In the short run, coaching may take up a lot of your time, but over time the overall management workload tends to decline as team members' confidence and skills increase.

Important additional benefits are that staff who are coached tend to have greater job satisfaction and an increased sense of ownership for their work.

Transitioning your approach towards a coaching style requires modifying the relationship between you and the team members. As a coach you are not so much the boss, as a resource for team members to use. Team members are expected to get on and do their work and choose when they come to you for help. In coming to you for help the individuals are expected to know what outcome is desired, but are struggling with how to get there. Your role is to help them find a route themselves.

Minor adjustments in your conversations with staff can change the whole nature of the relationship between a manager and team members. There is not much difference in the wording of *I think that won't work* and *why do you think that isn't working?* – and yet the former statement will encourage an individual to look to the manager for an answer whereas the latter will encourage the individual to find a solution for themselves.

Another advantage of coaching is that you, as manager, do not have to know the answer to every problem. The appropriate attitude for a coach is not *I know the answer,* but *I'm sure you know the answer.* In coaching you let go of responsibility for solving a problem, but you take responsibility for helping an individual to develop.

Coaching can be challenging for a manager. All managers find themselves in the situations in which they think *well, I might as well do the work myself.* As a coach you have to avoid this. Adopting a coaching style requires taking a degree of trust in your team members' capabilities and their willingness to be coached.

Coaching is powerful and an important part of a manager's skill set. If you do not know how to coach, then you should seek advice and training. One of the best ways of understanding coaching is to be coached yourself.

Is it ever right to be directive?

Coaching can sound wonderful, and its fans present it as the solution to every problem in the world. In reality, coaching is not always the ideal approach.

In high-pressure situations, with rapidly approaching deadlines, coaching may be a luxury you cannot afford. If a building is burning down you don't coach people out of the building, you just tell them to get out. Business deadlines are often like a burning building.

Additionally, coaching only works if an individual wants to be coached. People do not always respond well to coaching. There can sometimes be an attitude of *just give me the answer*. In these situations, it is usually best to persevere with coaching. However, the attitude of the team member must be to want to solve the problem. If the team member does not have the capability or desire to solve the issue, coaching will not work.

Managers sometimes avoid coaching because they feel they are working in a high-pressure situation, and team members do not have the capability to be coached. This is usually an excuse. Coaching takes time to get used to. Individuals who have never been coached find it peculiar at first. But with time they will get used to it and learn to appreciate it. If you never take the time to help your team members solve problems for themselves, you will find you never have the time. If you are overloaded, you will remain overloaded and involved in every problem in the team.

You can mix directive and coaching styles. You can think of the work of your team as conceptually made up of layers. The top layer is the goals to be achieved, the second layer is the work that must be done to achieve these goals, and the bottom layer is how this work is to be performed. You can mix being directive and coaching at different layers.

Applying this model, you may sometimes be totally directive about goals, what will achieve the goals and how the tasks are done. Alternatively, you may be directive about goals and what to do, but encourage team members to work out, with your coaching support, how to do it. Then again, you may be prescriptive about goals, but encourage team members to work out, with your coaching support, what to do and how to do it. Occasionally, you may not even be directive about goals – letting team members work out all the layers for themselves.

Effective management is not a matter of one style or another. It is a matter of the right style for the right situation. Too many managers rely on directive approaches and are insufficiently competent or confident in positioning themselves as a coach. Most teams need less detailed direction than their managers think.

Work on this more if ...

- You use only one style of intervention with staff.
- You cannot let go of tasks which are not part of the management workload.
- Your staff are not developing and have a high level of dependency on your personal expertise.

Manager's checklist

- Being directive is best in high-pressure situations with tight deadlines, and with staff who will not respond to coaching.
- A coaching approach helps your staff to develop and in time to become more independent and needing less management support.
- Coaching can seem like a lot of work, but the investment pays off in more self-sufficient team members in the longer run.
- You do not have to choose one or other approach; you can combine them.

No team is an island

What is this about and why is it important?

A business is made up of interacting teams with work flowing between them. These flows of work are your business processes. Depending on how well business processes are designed and operate, your life will be more or less difficult. Effective managers understand the details of a team's operations, but also periodically sit back to monitor how the team interrelates with the rest of the organisation. The effective manager actively seeks to influence the interaction between teams.

Your role is to develop a team not as an isolated island, but as an integral part of the organisation. If you focus purely on your team, you will tend to become isolated. With isolation you risk running an inefficient and irrelevant team. If you want your team's performance and value to the organisation to increase, you have to integrate successfully.

How important this is depends on your seniority. Senior managers typically spend more time worrying about end-to-end business processes, and less time on the detailed mechanics of the individual team's work, when compared to junior managers.

Objective for managers

- To optimise the value delivered by your team as an integral part of the organisation.

Common issues in achieving this objective

- Failure to see the business from an end-to-end perspective.
- Lack of political sensitivity or skills.

The management guide

Business processes

The work of every team is part of a business process. In business process thinking you interact with supplying teams who do preceding work and hand it over to you, and you interact with customer teams whom you hand over your work to, so they can do the following work. The process is bounded by external suppliers whom you buy products and services from, and by your external customers who buy a product or service from you. Between your external suppliers and external customers the work you do adds value. The added value is the basis of the business.

The quality and volume of work performed by your team is dependent on what is done by the teams who supply you. There are many aspects to good process design, but an essential principle is that the work reaching you (your inputs) should be of an acceptable quality. You should not be expending effort quality checking or re-doing work done by the team that supplies you. Having completed your work, what you hand over to the proceeding team (your outputs), should also be of adequate quality so that the following team can utilise your outputs and their inputs without checking or modification.

Deciding what a good output looks like requires understanding the needs of the team you hand over to. They are your customer. You will receive inputs that are suitable for you because the preceding team, your supplier, designs their outputs to meet your requirements. Good process design starts with the requirements of the final external customer who actually buys a product or service from you, and flows all the way back through the organisation to your external suppliers.

Some readers may be rolling their eyes at this point – this is basic process design. It is true that these principles of process design are nothing new, and have been preached as essential for decades. These principles exist in many more sophisticated versions, such as in Six Sigma with concepts like Voice of the Customer, which businesses have exerted huge effort and expenditure implementing.

However, in reality, it is still common to find business processes where at handovers between departments, the first thing the receiving department does is quality-check and improve the outputs received from the preceding department. This is done because of a lack of trust between teams, usually based on a history of poor work being handed over. This is wasteful. If it happens at several steps in a process, it is hugely wasteful.

This wastefulness is made worse if resources in the teams are uneven. You could find that some teams can produce x units of outputs, but the team utilising these outputs can only process $0.9x$ units of inputs, or vice versa. This results in a backlog with work piling up at some points, and at others staff twiddling their thumbs waiting. Such a backlog is due to a bottleneck. One powerful approach to process enhancement is called the Theory of Constraints (see p. 231), which focuses on identifying and eliminating such bottlenecks.

These sorts of problems can be resolved, or at least minimised, by detailed management, better process design and planning. However, as an individual manager you usually do not have the remit or the power to redesign the whole process and it may feel as if there is nothing you can do.

You cannot solve all process problems, but you can mitigate them. There are several things you can do:

- Work closely with your customers to produce outputs of appropriate formats, timings, volumes and quality to suit their team.

- Work closely with your suppliers to provide you with inputs of appropriate formats, timings, volumes and quality to suit your team.

- Lobby senior managers and process owners to redesign processes where there are regular problems.

- If you have the appetite, volunteer to run a process re-engineering team to resolve the problems end-to-end. But do not underestimate how much work this can be.

Initially, when processes are analysed, it can seem as if the whole process is broken with a myriad of problems. You cannot fix everything, so start with the biggest issues. Often, many identified problems are symptoms and not root causes of the process failures. If you dig deep enough you will often find one type of work, usually done towards the start of the process, that is the cause of the majority of problems further down. A classic example is the quality of orders created by the sales department. Fix the front end of most processes and the whole process will run more smoothly and efficiently.

The network of relationships

The need to work as part of a process, and to try and optimise the same process, is one example of a wider phenomenon in organisations. Your team is not a stand-alone entity – it has a network of interactions and relationships that are essential to your work being effective.

Many teams do not have one customer and one supplier and are not part of one process, but have many customers and suppliers and work as part of several processes. If the team you run is a support function, like IT or finance, the chances are you will be involved in many processes. In some situations teams that are your customers for one type of work will be suppliers for another. Unless you have a picture of these interactions you will struggle to run an effective value-adding team.

It's a political world

It is important to develop a very clear image of the position of your team in the organisation. This image can be described in the common diagrams of a business: organisation charts, process flows, systems architectures. This is the *technical image* of the business.

An important activity is to make sure that the technical images managers use are correct and commonly accepted. Often the reality of work is somewhat different from the official image, and various managers have diverse sets of perspectives.

However, in principle this technical image can be objective and common. The technical image can be designed and understood by rational thinking and analysis. It is the image of a business that works through input and outputs, volumes and forecasts, hierarchies and defined interfaces.

But there is another image of the business that the most effective managers are aware of. This is a *human image* of the business, described in terms of relationships, interests and personalities. Such images are subjective and unique to individuals. Separate managers may have similar human images, but they are never exactly the same. This is business as understood by emotional intelligence, and is awash with politics. It is a business that works through alliances, favours and selectively shared information. (See also the section 'Think networks, not hierarchies' on pp. 68–73.)

For example, at one level process redesign is a purely rational activity. But in reality, if a process is altered someone's power or resources will be altered. Someone will perceive themselves as a winner, and someone else a loser. The winner will tend to support the process redesign, the loser will tend to resist it. Unless you are alert to these kinds of human reaction to events you will struggle to survive beyond a certain level in an organisation.

Ideally, all managers in an organisation are aligned behind a common strategy and share common goals. But some managers will be your allies; others will have incompatible interests. These differences may be caused by poorly designed organisation, processes and systems. They may also be caused by dissimilar philosophies or approaches to work or personality clashes. You can reduce these incompatible interests, but you cannot remove them totally.

Dealing with the human side of business is often labelled as *politics,* and is usually regarded as a bad thing. The thinking goes that you should not involve yourself in politics and only devious characters do. This is naive. Politics is a natural part of human interaction. Certain political actions are wrong, but politics itself is an essential part of getting things done in organisations. If you

want to move to any level of seniority in management, then you
must learn to handle, and play a part in, organisational politics.

Work on this more if ...

- You do not know who your customers or suppliers are – or
  what their needs are.
- You regularly receive poor-quality and too many or too few
  inputs.
- You feel it essential to quality check and rework inputs
  handed over to you.
- You do not have adequate understandings of your
  organisation at the technical or human level.

Manager's checklist

- The work of your team is part of one or more processes.
  You should design your outputs to meet the needs of your
  customers, and demand inputs from your suppliers that enable
  you to achieve this.

- Managers should have two images of the business: a *technical
  image* of organisation charts, process flows and systems; and a
  human image of relationships, interests and personalities.

- Politics is not bad – it is an essential part of organisations.
  If you wish to become a senior manager you must develop
  political sensitivity and skills.

five

The productive team

Part 4 talked about the core basics of management: providing your team with a sense of direction and allocating work. Part 5 builds on this by exploring how you go beyond a team that is just busy to a team that is productively busy.

The first two sections of this part discuss the critical issues of motivation, progress tracking and performance management. The abilities to motivate a team, track progress and manage performance are essential for all managers.

The third section looks at a side issue, but an important one. Your team members have expectations and beliefs about what they are entitled to and what is fair treatment at work. As a manager your behaviour directly affects these expectations and beliefs. Where there is a mismatch between team member and manager expectations and beliefs there can be real difficulties. These difficulties can reduce team productivity significantly.

The final section discusses one of the tasks that seems

to eat up more time and resource in business than almost any other, and which is often a very unproductive use of time – meetings. Whilst many meetings are pointless, others are essential. The section explores what meetings you should run, and how you ensure they are productive.

Engaging and motivating the team

What is this about and why is it important?

It is frequently observed that people do not just come to work and perform at their highest levels. Some team members hardly perform at all, but others never have enough to do. There are large variations in capabilities, but if you take a sample of people with similar capabilities, the difference in performance levels is huge. Some of the main factors contributing towards these performance variations are the degrees of engagement and motivation.

Engagement results from the relationship between individual team members' beliefs and desires, and the nature of tasks and the goals of the team. *Motivation* results from the incentives offered to encourage people to perform. One helpful way to think is encapsulated in the definition of engagement as *intrinsic motivation* or *self-motivation*, and motivation as *extrinsic motivation*.

A significant influence on the levels of team member engagement and motivation is your behaviour, and how you seek to engage and motivate your team. You will get the best performance, and avoid many performance issues, if you have an engaged and motivated team. There can be orders-of-magnitude difference in terms of work completed and outcomes achieved between a well-motivated and a demotivated team.

Objectives for managers

- To understand engagement and align individuals with the most appropriate work.
- To achieve the best levels of motivation with the levers you have available to you.

Common issues in achieving these objectives

- Inappropriate selection of staff relative to activity and team or organisational goals.
- Inappropriate use, or non-availability, of motivational levers.
- Inadequate consideration given to engagement and motivation.

The management guide

You need to engage and motivate staff to reliably realise beneficial behaviour. What behaviour do you want team members to exhibit? The answer seems obvious: you want to maximise performance. But reasons for motivation can be more complex than this. For instance, you may also want to motivate people to stay with an organisation, reduce staff turnover and remove the cost and disruption of regular recruitment. Unless you know what behaviour you want to achieve, your motivation tactics may not work.

For simplicity's sake, I use the word *performance* to encompass any behaviour you want to encourage in your staff, but it should be borne in mind that this is shorthand for whatever outcome you want to achieve.

Engagement

Some individuals will naturally be engaged in the work of your team. They are attracted to the team, interested in their tasks, and find the success of the team or organisation appealing.

If you can allocate work such that team members are involved in activities they are naturally interested in or enjoy, they will tend to be self-motivated. Team members will want to be involved in and complete tasks for personal satisfaction. Engagement can also be achieved by offering people work which aligns with their values. The tasks may be less enjoyable, but if the tasks are directly contributing towards achieving a goal the team member strongly believes in, the team member will be engaged. This can be seen in often high levels of motivation in the voluntary and charitable sectors in the face of often relatively low financial rewards.

There are natural limitations to how much you can align the tasks people do with what they want to do. You cannot offer someone work they enjoy if the things they enjoy are not part of your team's workload. There will always be activities that must be performed that no one likes. Some tasks need expertise, and sometimes the only expert is not interested in the work. Most people's personal belief in the goals of a business is limited.

To some extent consistently communicating the right messages encourages team members to see their work as beneficial or aligned to their personal beliefs, but this only works to a certain degree. The best way to maximise engagement goes back to the recruitment process. There are significant advantages in selecting individuals for the team who enjoy the type of work you do (see pp. 32–7). Unfortunately, the recruitment process is not foolproof and sometimes you have to take candidates without ideal attitudes to work. But you should try to select the people who are most interested in your work. A candidate with an excessive interest in monetary rewards, who asks no questions about the content of the work during an interview, is unlikely to be engaged.

You can also achieve a level of engagement when the individual is less interested in the task at hand, but feels themselves to be part of a team they want to be part of. If your team has a strong positive sense of identity, individuals will tend to want to maximise the achievements of the team.

Motivation

Motivation is achieved by team members perceiving a relationship between the rewards they are offered and their performance. Rewards vary from praise and acknowledgement of someone's behaviour, to money, promotion and career enhancement. Whilst financial rewards are an important part of business and team member expectations, they are not the only motivators.

Motivational incentives are personal and individual. Everybody is motivated by different things. Although it is possible to make some generalisations about motivation, you have to be careful to avoid making too broad and invalid assumptions.

For an incentive to work there has to be a clear relationship between achievements attained and the reward offered. This relationship needs to be explicit to the individual whose behaviour you want to encourage. The challenge this brings is to balance the following:

- **Personal performance**: to maximise the performance of the individual, rewards have to be directly tied to the efforts or outcomes of the individual. The risk with excessive focus on personal behaviour is a lack of team play: for example, the sales manager who focuses on sales to achieve personal commission, but does not worry about the quality or appropriateness of sales made. Personal incentives are excellent if high individual performance is what you want. If you are trying to build a team, they are less helpful.

- **Team or company performance**: to maximise the performance of a team or company, rewards should be linked to team or company performance. There are two risks from this: firstly, the free rider who gets the reward based on everyone else's work; secondly, the high performers demotivated by seeing rewards averaged down to the mean performance of the team.

Generally, the right answer is to have a mix of incentives, some personal and some group. The best balance depends on the type of organisation, the role and what you are trying to achieve. There is no perfect answer, and organisations constantly tinker with incentive schemes.

There can be a temptation to devise ever more complex incentive schemes. A complex system can balance contending pressures, but is not without problems. Complex incentive schemes can be difficult and time consuming to maintain, and individuals can lose site of the connection between their performance and rewards.

You work with the processes, culture and norms of the business you are in. There may be many ideal ways of motivating your team, but you have to work with the motivation tools that are available within your business.

Financial rewards

Contrary to popular wisdom, financial rewards can be motivational. Some of your team members will improve their behaviour and performance for the opportunity of financial rewards.

However, purely financial incentives suffer from a number of problems. A common issue is that money becomes an expectation irrespective of performance, and is not perceived as a reward. Once this happens, money does not motivate people, but its absence becomes a demotivator.

The financial rewards you can offer will be limited. A business will offer certain mechanisms for motivating people, but restrict the use of others. For example, one business may offer bonuses but no share options; another offers share options but no bonuses.

Even with pay rises you are constrained as a manager. You may have some freedom, for instance to allocate the annual increase in salary budget as you like to your team. If your total budget increase is only 1%, the opportunity to give any one individual a large pay rise is restricted. Additionally, pay rises are normally once a year. If some significant achievement happens early in the year, rewarding it almost a year later has limited positive behavioural impact.

People have different thresholds and are satisfied at different salary levels. For one person a salary of £40,000 is enough; for another it is an unacceptably low amount. For those who are motivated by money, the bigger the salary, the bigger the increase that is needed to become a motivator. For someone earning £20,000, the chance of earning an extra 5% or £1,000 may be a reasonable motivator. For someone on £250,000, £1,000 is irrelevant and even 5% may not mean much as the impact on the lifestyle of a person earning that much money is negligible.

Hence you get the scenario of vast bonuses for people on huge salaries.

Non-financial rewards

Do not get fixated on financial rewards. Many of the best motivators do not cost you anything and often it is the non-financial rewards that an individual manager has most leeway to offer.

People are generally more motivated if work is fun. Some organisations focus on making the environment relaxed, friendly and fun. Such companies often have high performance, whilst paying lower than average salaries. Not every manager is a natural joker, but if you are not, you can encourage humour in your team members.

People are more likely to be motivated if they feel respected, and if they perceive their work and individual contribution is valued. Regular, positive feedback will do as much as many financial incentives.

If you do want to give rewards, consider giving very small gifts, linked to particular events and activities and given quickly after the event or activity is complete; this will have as significant an effect as an annual pay rise given months after activities are ended. Examples include meals out, trophies, vouchers, award ceremonies or any other small, but appreciated, gift.

Be creative in the non-financial rewards you offer. Vary them, so they do not become expectations. Give them frequently, and soon after you have observed the behaviour or performance you want to encourage.

Work on this more if ...

- You are recruiting new members into your team.
- You have low levels of motivation in your team.

Manager's checklist

- Select team members who are naturally engaged in the work you do.

- You have to work within the motivational levers available.

- For an incentive to work there has to be a clear linkage to the performance you want to encourage.

- Balance individual incentives with team or group incentives.

- Financial rewards can be motivators, but they need careful handling. There are limitations on your power to offer them.

- Non-financial rewards are highly effective. Be creative – many different ones are available to you.

Keeping on track

What is this about and why is it important?

Your team will not always complete the work you ask them to do. Instructions will be misinterpreted, problems will arise, and people will need help. Regularly, some team members will not perform at the expected levels.

Activity needs to be monitored to confirm it is happening at the required pace, and being undertaken to appropriate levels of quality. The type and frequency of monitoring depends on the individuals being monitored and the nature of the task. Experienced and reliable team members working on familiar tasks need limited monitoring. Less experienced and new team members, those with a history of poor performance, or those working on unusual tasks need more. This process of monitoring activity is called *progress tracking*.

Progress tracking is a continuous activity focused on the short term. It provides the information for the longer-term process of *performance management*. Performance management includes assessments of team member's work, as well as objective setting, staff development, promotion and rewards. Additionally, performance management provides mechanisms for dealing with performance problems. The term *performance management* is often used as a euphemism for handling poorly performing and difficult staff, including terminating employment.

Team performance is your responsibility. You control who is in the team and what they do. With performance management you have the tools to motivate and reward staff, and to exclude staff who are unable or unwilling to perform at necessary levels. Effective performance management is demanding and requires vigilance and consistency. Ignore performance management tasks for an extended period, and you risk causing trouble for yourself and your business.

Objectives for managers

- A team that performs at a constantly high level.
- Individuals whose skills are continuously being enhanced.
- Team member goals which are consistent with business objectives.

Common issues in achieving these objectives

- Ineffective progress tracking.
- Intensive workload limits time for performance management.
- Desire to avoid uncomfortable conversations and an inability to give effective feedback when discussing performance.

The management guide

Progress tracking

Progress tracking is the regular monitoring of the advances team members make in their assigned work. Progress tracking is undertaken:

- To gain confidence in your team's progress on current work.
- To understand team members' capabilities.
- To provide information for management reporting.
- To enable appropriate management interventions to redirect work and provide support to team members when necessary.

Monitoring is easier if the work being done is visible and measurable. If a task creates a widget it's straightforward to measure how many widgets are made. It becomes more difficult with many tasks associated with services or professional skills. For example, tracking how much of a design has been completed and assessing the quality of the design is much harder.

When you allocate tasks always plan how you are going to track progress. Often the only way to understand progress is by

entering into detailed dialogue with the team members responsible for the work. Such detailed conversations may need to be
scheduled in advance. If performance tracking is complex and
onerous, you should make reporting on the task part of the work.

With progress tracking you want to avoid the feeling that you are
being overly controlling or constantly on people's backs. If team
members perceive your management as overbearing, productivity can decline. However, even reliable team members have to
recognise your need to track progress, if for no other reason than
your need to do management reporting.

There is little point in tracking progress unless you take action,
or management interventions, based on the information you
gather. This action can be as simple as praising high performance, and encouraging poorly performing staff to do better.
But management intervention can include redirecting team
members if your instructions were misunderstood, allocating
additional resource when work is proving troubling, or helping
team members to overcome barriers to progress.

Although there is always an element of progress tracking that
ensures staff do what they were told to do, this should be a
minor part. The most productive attitude is to consider progress
tracking as the mechanism by which you understand how to
help your staff best.

Progress tracking can place the emphasis on activity and being
busy. Always remember that it is not being busy that counts, but
achieving goals.

Performance management

Performance management is the name for the longer-term processes
for encouraging appropriate performance and providing team
members with the support they need to develop personally.
The basis for performance management is the history of information from progress tracking. Performance management entails
rewarding good performance, and sometimes penalising poor
performance.

Performance management is normally undertaken according to processes defined by the HR department. If it is done well, performance management helps businesses, teams and individuals, by bringing alignment between the objectives of the individual and the business. Although it is team performance that really matters, performance management focuses on the individual.

Theoretically, there are four alternative outcomes from performance management:

- Improvement in individual performance.
- Maintaining consistent and acceptable performance.
- Change of role, due to good or poor performance.
- Exit of an individual from an organisation for poor performance.

Improving individual performance is the primary goal of performance management. However, some individuals reach a point in their career when their performance plateaus. In such cases, performance management should focus on maintaining the current level of performance and avoiding any decline.

A common outcome of performance management is a change of role. This may be a promotion, or it may be moving someone to a role which is more suited to their aspirations and skills. Performance management enables managers to understand their staff better and staff to understand roles better. With improved understanding by both sides, it's easier to identify members of staff who would be better off in different roles. Usually, this is in the business's interest too.

Finally, sometimes individuals have to exit the organisation due to poor performance. Ideally this is mutually agreed. But sometimes it requires firing someone. This is a protracted and often unpleasant course of action. It is often avoidable if early enough interventions are made to help individuals. Unfortunately, many managers delay intervening when they become aware of poor performance.

Do not postpone dealing with performance problems – it never helps. If you let a performance problem carry on without intervention you are complicit in it. You have allowed the expectation to grow that you find the performance acceptable. This makes dealing with problems far harder.

The performance management process is time consuming, but essential. Having a record of accurate documented performance reports will make your life easier in the longer run. Whether it is justifying promotions or more difficult decisions such as redundancy and dismissal, a complete set of accurate performance reports is indispensable.

Feedback

Progress tracking activities and performance reviews should result in feedback. Feedback is simply providing information to your team members so they know what behaviour to start or continue and what behaviour to stop. Feedback is an incredibly simple and powerful mechanism. But it is one that many managers struggle with. Yet there are some straightforward guidelines for feedback which can make it effective.

Effective feedback is specific and actionable. Avoid general statements. Comments like *generally your performance is good*, or *you are not really up to the mark*, are not helpful. The purpose of feedback is to encourage or discourage specific behaviour. You do this by pinpointing the precise behaviour in question, and explaining the impact of it in a way that encourages individuals to modify or repeat behaviour depending on the situation.

Feedback should be timely. Preferably, it is given as soon as possible after you have observed the behaviour you want to encourage or discourage. Don't wait for performance reviews to give feedback. Performance reviews are infrequent – sometimes quarterly, and for many people only annually. Immediate feedback is effective. Feedback given weeks or months after an event is largely pointless.

Feedback should be regular. If you make feedback regular it is less likely to seem like criticism and more likely to be taken as constructive help. Also by regular feedback you create a culture in which feedback becomes part of the normal process of work.

Finally, feedback should point at behaviour, not the individual. You do not accuse an individual of doing something wrong – you help by indicating which behaviour is not to be repeated.

Objective setting

To assess someone's performance you need a definition of expected performance. This is given by objectives. A central part of performance management is objective setting.

Good objectives are mutually agreed, clear, achievable but demanding, and measurable. Objectives must be aligned to the needs of the business, and ideally the desires of individual team members. For objectives to be effective, they have to be lived – directly influencing the behaviour of team members on an ongoing basis.

Objective setting can be thought of as a negotiation between yourself as the manager and each member of your team. The aim of this negotiation is not to get the best deal for the business or the individual, but to align objectives in such a way that the business gets what it wants from the individual, and the individual gets what he or she wants from the business.

You can also think of objective setting as a way to gain understanding and set expectations. By defining objectives you set the expectations of the business. In discussion team members explain their desires and aspirations. Effective objective setting is a dialogue between manager and team member. It is not a directive from the firm of the form *you must achieve this*, or a wish list from the team member in the form of *I want to get this*. Of course, you cannot always give team members objectives they want.

Objectives should be a living part of the daily work of the team. There is a risk that achieving objectives is seen as something extra and different from everyday work. The subsequent risk is that objectives are forgotten and only thought about in the few weeks running up to the annual appraisal.

The distributed team

Geographically distributed teams pose particular problems for progress tracking and performance management. Performance management requires dialogue and is aided by relationships. Progress tracking requires evidence. All of these things are helped by face-to-face interaction and observation of team members at work.

If you run a distributed team you have to put more effort into relationship building and communicating with team members. Relationships that would develop and dialogue that would occur if the team were physically in one place, require deliberate planning and action.

Make as many opportunities for face-to-face contact as practical, even if you have to go out of your way. Where one-to-one, face-to-face communication is not possible, use whatever is the next most intimate communications medium. Avoid relationships that only exist through email.

Work on this more if ...

- You struggle assessing progress.
- You are uncomfortable giving feedback.
- Your team members have inappropriate objectives.

Manager's checklist

- Progress tracking enables you to understand how to help your team to complete the work assigned to them in the best manner.

- Keep on top of performance management. It is time-consuming, but accurate performance records are essential for effective management.

- Effective feedback is specific, actionable, timely and regular and concerns behaviour rather than people.

■ The best objectives are agreed, clear, achievable but demanding, measurable, and aligned to the needs of the business and the desires of individual team members.

■ Geographically distributed teams pose challenges for progress tracking and performance management which managers must strive to overcome.

Entitlement and fairness: reasonableness and imbalances

What is this about and why is it important?

The desire to be treated fairly is innate to humans. Being treated unfairly is regarded as wrong. Individuals who act unfairly are considered as unethical. An important aspect of fairness is receiving your due entitlements. Entitlements at work include pay and benefits, but there are many other rights.

Fairness and a respect for entitlements are important for managers to observe. Fairness is required for ethical reasons and to remain legally compliant. Everyone has a right to receive what they are entitled to. These points seem so reasonable that it is difficult to imagine any problem.

The challenge for managers is that fairness is a subjective concept. Imbalances arise between the views of members of the team, managers and the wider organisation. One person's view of absolute fairness is seen by another as complete unreasonableness.

It might be thought that the situation is clearer with entitlements. Many entitlements are contractual obligations between the employee and the employer. In this case, it should be clear what is and is not a valid entitlement. But even here subjective judgement comes into play. Expectations of future benefits can easily turn into beliefs of entitlements, or rights to rewards. Unless these expectations are consistent between team members and managers there is a risk of conflict.

In practice, failure to manage expectations or meet entitlements, and failure to be seen to be fair cause many disputes at work.

Objectives for managers

- To be seen to treat team members fairly, whilst being able to respond to their differing needs and take advantage of their different capabilities.

- To ensure team members get what they are entitled to whilst avoiding developing increasing expectations and a creeping expansion of entitlements.

Common issues in achieving these objectives

- Fairness is a subjective perception of a state of affairs. A manager may believe he is acting fairly whilst a team member regards herself as subject to unfair treatment.

- The behaviour of managers can inadvertently lead to beliefs in entitlements and perceptions of unfair treatment.

The management guide

Fairness and entitlement are moving targets. Managers should consider several issues. Firstly, you will be judged on people's perception of how fairly you treat individuals and how well you ensure staff get what they are entitled to. Secondly, your judgement of what is fair and what staff are entitled to will often be different from the perspectives of team members. Thirdly, the way you act, decisions you make and the expectations you set will affect team members' judgements of what is fair and what they are entitled to.

Perceptions of unfairness

Let's look at a way you can create an accusation of unfairness. Imagine you do one member of staff a favour, which you perceive purely as a good turn. Perhaps you let someone go home early one day. Maybe you are more flexible to one member of staff because of something happening in their private life. Or you let one member of staff work in an office whilst everyone else sits in the open-plan space. The examples are endless.

You cannot see how anyone else can worry about this. After all nobody is actually worse off just because you have done something for another member of the team. This is true – but people will perceive they are worse off. Offering one person trivial help, favours, benefits, can be seen as favouritism or unfairness. Managers are often surprised, even shocked, when an accusation of unfairness arises. The thoughts that go through the manager's head are 'be reasonable' or 'don't be so childish'.

These are understandable thoughts, but then think of children. If none of your children has sweets then they are all happy. But give one child sweets and any other child will be upset if they are not offered them as well. The hurtful feeling from being treated unfairly runs deep and cannot be removed by the logical argument – *well you are no worse off because I gave Charlie some sweets*. It is no different at work. The need for fairness does not disappear with age.

Worse, a perception of unfairness can turn into a claim for discrimination. What you perceive to be helping out a member of the team is seen as favouritism. It is not a long ride from favouritism to claims of discrimination. Discrimination claims can be difficult to prove false, will reduce your confidence, will be hurtful – and may damage your career.

But aren't we all different?

One challenge is that uniform treatment is not efficient or effective. It is not even right to treat everyone the same.

Everyone is different and has different needs and different criteria about what they value. One member of staff values flexibility in working hours, another wants overtime to maximise their pay packet. One wants private health care, another prefers a higher take-home pay package. One wants an easy life, another will do anything to maximise career prospects. One hates the Christmas party and prefers a gift voucher.

People have varying skills and abilities. It is appropriate, and even necessary, to treat them differently. You want to promote high-flyers and give them opportunities to learn in challenging circumstances. Other members of the team need to be focused on following a steady routine. A routine they perform well, but do not cope well outside of. And there will be a group that needs to be constantly monitored and helped to even do the basic tasks you expect.

Creating expectations and entitlements

Beliefs in entitlement come about from habits. No matter what the contract says, if you pay staff a non contractual bonus every year for ten years, in the eleventh when you do not there will be trouble. Just saying, *well it was never contractual*, does little to help.

Many of the perceptions of entitlement come from minor incentives. Give a small prize every month for the best-performing member of the team, and it will soon become an assumed entitlement. Another example is the Christmas party. It is amazing how upset people get if the Christmas party is cancelled. The Christmas party for many is considered a right. This type of small right may not matter much, but the cumulative effect of many is expensive and much worse, creates inflexibility and points of resistance to change.

How did you get to this state? The Christmas party happens every year and is expected every year. Over time the expectation turns into a perceived entitlement. Once this has happened, if you stop it, then people see it as you removing their right.

Entitlements can also arise from what you do not make staff do. If you consistently do not enforce something staff should do, it can become, in time, an entitlement not to do it. The following pattern develops: you cannot be bothered to enforce the activity, gradually the activity stops being seen as necessary – it becomes something additional that needs to be negotiated or paid for before anyone will do it. Once you have reached that stage you have an entitlement. Enforce it and motivation dips. At worst you have industrial action. This is rare, but happens.

Avoiding problems

There are no silver bullets that will resolve all issues with unfairness or entitlement. The most important thing is to be conscious of the risk and try to anticipate problems arising in future. However, do not be obsessively risk-averse. Your team members do not expect you to be perfect and will have some tolerance for unfairness and changes to perceived entitlements. Sometimes, you just have to have a dispute. But if you use a bit of common sense you can avoid too many problems.

You must be even-handed to team members. But even-handedness does not mean uniform treatment for everyone. The following points give you some guidance to avoid perceptions of unfairness:

- When an individual or group is to be treated in a different fashion then ensure the rest of the team know why they have been treated differently. If the same conditions arise for other team members, then treat them in the same way.

- When applicable, offer everyone the same range of benefits and let them choose what they want. If people themselves choose different things, the perception of unfairness declines.

- Sometimes you need to be demanding and place pressure on team members. You will get away with this if you are even-handed and do this to all team members. However, if you consistently put pressure on only one or a few members of the team – that is bullying.

- Differentiate between childish complaints and valid concerns regarding unfairness. Ignore the former, but keep your ears open for the latter. If you have been unfair in a significant fashion try to redress the balance.

- Be alert and minimise the number of times you are accidentally unfair. No one is perfect, and most teams will forgive a certain amount, but every time you are unfair you are confronting a basic human need.

If you are happy to develop an entitlement – do it. The point is not to get there by accident. Tips concerning entitlements include:

- Avoid developing undesired entitlements in the first place. This is far easier than taking them away once the belief has been created.

- When you do give people something extra, make clear it is a one-off and for special circumstances. Regularly remind people it may be removed at a later date. This will not always stop habits developing, but it does help if disputes start.

- Minimise habits. Do good turns for your staff. But don't consistently do the same good turn for the same reason. Be innovative and creative in your benefits. This reduces expectations, and reduces the risk of developing a belief in an entitlement.

- Occasionally, but regularly, enforce the tedious parts of the job that often get forgotten. If you never do, eventually you will not be able to do it without a fight.

Work on this more if ...

- There is a perception of unfair treatment in your team.
- You are constantly fighting expectations and increasing belief in entitlements.

Manager's checklist

- Be conscious of the risk of acting unfairly and developing entitlements.

- Apply common and explicit principles, but interpret them according to individuals' needs and capabilities.

- Avoid habitual extra benefits, unless you want to develop an entitlement. Offer extras, but change them around regularly.

- From time to time, enforce every part of a job. If you don't, eventually you won't be able to.

The curse and delight of meetings

What is this about and why is it important?

Ask many people what they most dislike about work, and there is a fair chance the answer will be meetings. Meetings fill up diaries so there is no time for 'real work'. Meetings are boring and sap energy. Meetings eat up resources. Meetings are seen as pointless and painful conventions that businesses seem unnecessarily addicted to.

It does not have to be like this. It is true that many meetings are ineffective. It is also true that people waste huge amounts of time in non-productive meetings. The easy conclusion is that meetings are the problem. This conclusion is wrong. The problems are:

- Poor assessments of which meetings are worthwhile, combined with a tendency to see meetings as the solution to all problems. This leads to too many worthless meetings.
- Poor skills in managing meetings. This leads to those boring, energy-sapping, pointless, painful and unproductive events.

Meetings are an essential part of business. Business is not made up of individuals working in isolation. It is made up of people working together in a coordinated fashion. This requires interaction – and an important forum for interaction is the meeting. You will spend a significant proportion of your working life in meetings.

Managers have a central role in ensuring the right meetings take place in the right way. If you do this you will make your team more effective and efficient. As an added benefit, if you manage to weed out the pointless and badly run meetings, you will also be popular.

Objective for managers

- To have productive and enjoyable meetings – the right meetings run in the right way.

Common issues in achieving this objective

- Meetings are part of the culture and ritual of business. As such they often go unchallenged.
- Meetings become fixed parts of schedules and carry on long beyond their useful life.
- Meetings are often badly run. Few people know how to run meetings well.

The management guide

There are good and bad reasons for having meetings. There are good and bad ways of running meetings. Bad meetings and badly run meetings are one of the curses of business. The right meetings, run well, can be one of the delights of business.

The format of meetings is expanding. We still have face-to-face meetings, but there are teleconferences, videoconferences, mobile meetings and online meetings. New technology will continue to give us more options. The increase of geographically spread teams, especially those working in different time zones, has placed extra pressures on meetings. But the fundamental principles of effective meetings still hold.

When should you hold meetings?

Meetings are an essential part of management. If you are not meeting people, and meeting them regularly, then it is questionable what you are doing as a manager. Most managers could probably use their time more efficiently if they reduced the number of meetings they attend. But even so, meetings of one form or another will remain a significant proportion of a manager's working time.

The only time to hold a meeting is when you have a reason to. If you do not have a clear reason for holding a meeting then don't hold one. That is not to say that meetings cannot be used when goals are imprecise or vague, but then the reason for the meeting should be to discuss and clarify goals.

There are many bad reasons for holding meetings, including:

- Sharing information which can effectively be emailed to everyone or put on the Web.

- Disseminating information that can be shared quickly and efficiently by a phone call, as you walk around the office or stand by the coffee machine.

- Discussing information and topics that need significant analysis and time for reflection. A meeting might be used to introduce the topics, or review conclusions, but meetings are not great periods for reflection.

- Habit: because you always have a meeting at this time, or there is a regular invitation in your diary.

- You are not sure what to do and a meeting feels comforting as at least you are doing something.

- You just feel like it.

A variation on this is when there are reasons for a meeting, but there is no reason for *you* to be there. Only go to meetings that are useful to you or you can usefully contribute to. Only send your team members to meetings that are useful to themselves or the team or which they can usefully contribute to. Unfortunately, you cannot escape all pointless meetings. Some you just have to go to. Your boss may insist on your attendance at certain meetings. This is one of those things you just have to accept in business. But you should seek to minimise it.

However, there are good reasons to hold meetings. Hold meetings when:

- A topic needs discussion amongst a group of people, especially when interaction is required.

- You want to build relationships between people.

- When you need to see or hear people's reactions. (Email is a very poor substitute.)
- When information may create a response that needs immediate management.
- When it is respectful to say what you need to say face-to-face.

How to hold meetings

Meetings come to be faced with dread, but meetings can be productive and fun. Factors which contribute towards effective meetings are:

- What is best done outside the meeting is done outside the meeting, e.g. pre-reading is handed out and read, preparation work is completed.
- Having a shared understanding of the objective of the meeting. What is the purpose of the meeting and how will a meeting achieve that purpose?
- Someone is nominated to run or facilitate the meeting.
- There is a process for the meeting. This can be as simple as an agenda to follow or it can be as complex as a team of professional facilitators running a workshop. The process should be structured, but should not be an end in itself. Overly onerous processes kill creativity and energy.
- An appropriate length of time is allocated. Not too long and not too short. If a long time is needed it should be broken into shorter chunks of no more than an hour.
- The right group of people is available. Normally there is a compromise, but enough people of sufficient knowledge and authority to achieve the desired outcome should be present. If you can't get them, don't go ahead with the meeting.
- Ideally, the attenders are respectful of each other. They do not have to agree, but they should listen to each other even if it gets heated.

Understand your own role. Are you the chairman or an expert contributor? There is a tendency for managers to assume they have to chair their team meetings. You do not have to and it is not always best. It is hard to run a meeting effectively and be a contributor – and sometimes your main interest is as a contributor. Also, some managers simply do not make good meeting chairs. If your meeting needs a chair and you are not the right person, pick someone else from your team to run the meeting. It's a useful development opportunity.

You cannot always control the environment for your meeting. If you can, it helps a lot. Choose an environment in which:

- You can concentrate.
- You are unlikely to be able to drift off.
- You don't get interrupted or distracted.

I personally like the stand-up meeting. It can be very fast and effective. It is impossible to fall asleep and no one talks for too long.

A rather obvious, but often forgotten point – meetings need to end. The process for managing the meeting should bring it to clear conclusion. If the goal of the meeting cannot be achieved, for example consensus is not achieved, then alternative steps should be agreed before ending the meeting.

Finally, the effectiveness of meetings is not just about what happens in the meeting, but what happens afterwards. All sorts of promises are given, actions are allocated, agreements are made. There must be a culture of fulfilling whatever was agreed in the meeting. Not doing this makes meetings a waste of time. It is also disrespectful of the attenders.

Helping your team with meetings

If you want to make your team more productive, one of the easiest things to do is to question the meetings they attend and to try and make the essential meetings more productive.

When you are in meetings observe how your team members behave there. Praise good meeting behaviour – don't just take it for granted. Where behaviour is less effective, coach your team members in better ways. If there is no other option, send them on meeting skills training courses.

Particularly stress the value of listening skills. Sometimes senior people talk and present ideas. But some of the most powerful and successful people spend most of their time in meetings listening. Your team members can learn from this.

Using limited learning and development opportunities or training budgets on meeting skills development may seem a waste. It is not.

Work on this more if ...

- You constantly find yourself in meetings which are pointless or ineffective.
- Your team members spend an inordinate amount of time in meetings.
- Nothing results from the meetings you hold.

Manager's checklist

- Only let meetings take place if there is an appropriate reason for the meeting to take place.
- If a meeting is needed, make sure it is structured and planned in the right way.
- Treat meeting skills as core skills for all your team members to develop.

six

The working manager

So far we have looked at shaping your role, working with a team and ensuring the team is productive. The focus was outwards towards a range of stakeholders, and more specifically the team, and on your work in helping the team to perform. In this and the following parts we shift the emphasis towards you and the activities you are personally responsible for.

The four topics dealt with in this part include decision making, prioritisation, overcoming barriers and problems in the team's work, and dealing with change. These are all activities that your team will look to you as the manager to perform. You can choose to involve team members in these activities, and in some situations you can delegate aspects of them. However, you as a manager remain the accountable owner for these activities. If you ask team members to record what they expect from their manager, activities like decision making and setting priorities will always appear high on their lists.

The topics which this part focuses on are the bread and butter work of the manager. Even dealing with change is a regular activity. Later parts will help you excel as a manager, and explain some of the skills that come with experience. The topics in this part should be seen as fundamental to all competent managers.

The crunch: making decisions

What is this about and why is it important?

Decision making is one of the essential skills for managers. All managers need to make decisions. Your performance as a manager is directly linked to your ability to make good decisions. For many managers a large part of the day is made up of identifying issues, assessing options and making decisions. Arguably, managers are paid as much for their decision-making ability as for anything else.

However, making decisions is one of the aspects of management that many people find difficult and stressful. *What if I make the wrong decision?* Don't worry. In most cases it is not that difficult or risky.

Objectives for managers

- To make effective decisions, appropriately, rapidly, and without excessive resource applied to the decision-making process.
- To encourage appropriate levels of delegated decision making within the team.

Common issues in achieving these objectives

- People do not know how to make decisions and do not like making decisions for fear of getting them wrong.
- Managers do not have sufficient information or time to make optimal decisions.
- Managers become overburdened with decision making.

The management guide

There is an infinite variety of decisions for managers: decisions needed to achieve the team's goals, decisions team members need to do their individual jobs, decisions about yourself and your career. Examples include: choosing team members, prioritisations, determining performance appraisals and feedback, and even selecting office layouts or furniture. Decisions can be trivial or profound, complex or simple, risky or harmless. Decision making is continuous and unavoidable.

There are theoretical approaches to decision making. We can read such explanations and see the unquestionable logic of listing the options, deciding the criteria to make a decision about, and then selecting the best option based on the criteria we have listed. All very nice, but the real world is somewhat different:

- There is never enough information. You won't know all the options or all the outcomes or fully understand the context.
- There may not be enough time to assess the available information.
- Gaining more information takes time and uses up resource that could be used for more productive things.
- As you analyse information the world moves on. Unless you are quick, you will be making an out-of-date decision.

Good decision making starts by framing the decision. By 'framing' I mean understanding precisely what the decision is. At this stage don't think about the options, context or associated issues. Just clarify the decision you need to make. A good approach is to frame a decision in terms of a simple question. If such a question has the word 'and' in it several times then it is not one decision, but several. If you cannot frame the decision, spend more time thinking about it. This will be more valuable than analysis of any other information. Examples of clear decisions are: should I do task A or task B first? Which supplier shall we use for the new contract? Should I recruit an extra team member?

Once you can frame your decision, consider two things.

Firstly, does this decision need to be made now? If a decision can be left without impacting anything else, then leave it for the time being. You have better things to do now. You will have more information in future and more time to think about it.

Secondly, do not assume all decisions are yours to make. Not all decisions need to, can or should be made by you. Forget the heroic manager who eats decisions for breakfast, lunch and tea. You have a team. They have expertise. Sometimes more than you do. Get them to do some of the work. Not only will you reduce your own burden, but you will help them to learn and develop. Put simply, you need to quickly decide what things you need to decide on.

Of course, there are appropriate and inappropriate decisions for team members to make, but team members should make many decisions themselves. Sometimes they will struggle. Give them a little assistance if they need it. But avoid giving them the answer all the time. If you do, do not be surprised if over time team members make fewer and fewer decisions and place more of the burden of decision making on your back.

However, some decisions need to be made immediately, quickly and by you.

Don't worry. Decisions are not frightening ogres. Decision making is nothing new – you have done it every day of your life. Perhaps not as a manager, but still you have lots of experience.

Most of the decisions you will make will be relatively small. Don't get stressed about small decisions. For most of the decisions you make on a daily basis the vital thing is *to make a decision*. Progress is often more important than which option you select. In many cases, you will not make the wrong choice, but may not make the optimal choice. Also, to be honest, often no one will know whether the choice made was for the best or not.

There is a human tendency to delay decision making. We may get fixated on the risk of making the wrong decision. For those who are risk-averse there is an uncomfortable truth to learn: there is a cost to *not* making or to delaying a decision as well as to making the wrong one. In business the cost of not making a decision is often higher than the cost of making the wrong decision.

You must strive for a balance in terms of speed and accuracy of decision making. You should not feel pressurised into making decisions just because it would make the life of someone in your team easier. On the other hand, it is reasonable for your boss and your team to expect you to make decisions quickly and effectively.

Categorise decisions into those that make a critical difference and those that just need to be made. The essential question is: *what is the risk and cost of getting this decision wrong?* Focus on those decisions where the risk and cost are high. Worry about those where the risk and cost are high, and the ones concerning something you are unfamiliar with or have limited expertise in.

For the others, don't agonise, just make a decision. Watch the outcome. If it does not work – amend your decision. Never be afraid of changing your mind or losing face. The only people who worry about losing face are those who have a reason to. You don't – as long as your decision making improves over time and you don't make the same mistakes twice.

If you have experience, rely on your intuition for the decisions you make regularly. You will find you get most right. The trick to effective management decision making is not to learn better algorithms or decision calculus – it is to improve your intuition.

Over time the cumulative effect of all the small decisions you make will be as important as those occasionally large ones. Therefore concern yourself with the overall direction and progress of the team rather than worrying too much if you should buy one or two packets of printer paper. In most cases if you observe the trend in what is happening in your team, then you will have time to fix those decisions that you get wrong.

Now this is not to say that there are no big and important decisions that you need to get right. These are the decisions to worry about and even occasionally to feel a little stressed over. Such decisions do not come along every day. In making such decisions:

- Make sure you can frame the decision properly.
- Work on this decision first. The earlier you start, the more time you have to think about it. Don't ignore it – it probably will not go away.
- Get help – this is the time to use your team, peers and boss for advice. Somebody will know more about this than you and will be able to help.
- Look for more information. Keep clear what the decision is, and why it is important. Sometimes more information makes you lose sight of the decision.
- If you can, share the risk. Ask someone else to confirm or approve your decision. Be wary of doing this too often as it looks like weakness. But now and again, involve your boss and be open that you do not know the answer. Get him or her to underwrite your decision.

Occasionally, there will be no right choice, only the least wrong one. When this happens manage your stakeholders' expectations by communicating that there will not be a perfect result from the decision. If they disagree, try and involve them in the decision-making process so they buy in to the answer.

Finally, don't fall over on assumptions. It is perfectly reasonable, and sometimes essential, to make assumptions before making a decision. But understand your assumptions and understand the risk associated with them being wrong. Do not simply write them down and then forget about them. If the assumption is unreasonable, or highly likely to be at error, your decision is likely to be poor.

Work on this more if …

- Decision making is slow and work is delayed constantly waiting for your decisions.
- Your ability to make decisions is the bottleneck to progress in the team.
- You are constantly making yesterday's decisions – not those for today or tomorrow.

■ Your decision making is not getting better with practice.

■ You find decision making stressful and worry about the decisions you make on a daily basis.

Manager's checklist

■ Frame the decision – express it as a simple, clear question.

■ Make sure it needs to be made now, and made by you.

■ For the small daily decisions, make them quickly, relying on your intuition. Over time observe the trend in outcomes and adjust your decisions if things can be improved.

■ Identify and expend most effort on the high-risk, high-cost decisions, especially those related to topics you have limited expertise in.

Are you really prioritising?

What is this about and why is it important?

Prioritisation is crucial for effective management. You and each of your team members should know your priorities. The need to prioritise comes from having insufficient resource to do all the possible work. Without coordinated priorities, a team will be inefficient – often, extremely inefficient.

Occasionally, you may think you have enough resources to do everything. Prioritisation is still needed. Some tasks bring significantly more benefit than others, and consequently should be done first. Also, this state never lasts for long. If you find yourself with such a breathing space, start thinking about future priorities.

Even resource-rich organisations have more activities that could be undertaken than they have resources to do. Prioritisation is hard in these environments. The demanding process of deciding where to allocate resources and what not to do is often ducked as a painful job that can be avoided. This results in wasted resources. But some managers prefer this to the difficult task of making choices.

Prioritisation is a form of decision making. Prioritisation decisions have to take account of contending business needs: for example, balancing doing today's work, keeping some powerful stakeholder happy, fixing short-term problems or achieving the longer-term visions. In prioritising, you are seeking to allocate your limited team resources to the most important needs. Prioritisation brings together all aspects of your team's role.

Objectives for managers

- To provide clarity for team members on what is important and what is not, and in which order activities should be completed.

- To ensure team members complete the most important tasks first.

- To give team members an ability to decide on the priority of their own workload without repeated recourse to the manager for detailed guidance.

Common issues in achieving these objectives

- Prioritisation is regularly not done at all.

- Prioritisation is perceived as too hard to do, especially in complex and volatile environments where you risk spending more time collecting information and prioritising than actually doing work.

- When it is done, prioritisation is often done ineffectively.

The management guide

Unfortunately, there is no painless way to prioritise. It takes effort, and an understanding of options and resource constraints. Although prioritisation requires analysis, it is above all an exercise in decision making – and many people find making choices difficult. Even when the choice is obvious, it may mean an uncomfortable decision resulting in some dissatisfied stakeholders.

Your precise role depends on your seniority, type of team and business culture, and the degree to which decision making is decentralised. Before starting to prioritise reflect on how much discretion you have. Are you making priorities or are you simply a channel for your boss's demands? Most of us have limits to our discretionary powers. If you are just a priorities communication channel to your team, you need to start by knowing your boss's mind.

However, let's assume you have to define priorities. Usually this means translating a broad sense of direction, or strategy, into a detailed instruction for your team. The logic of prioritisation is straightforward. List the possible tasks. Work out how important each task is, and then do them in the order of the most important first and least important last. Success in prioritisation is not starting the most important task first. It is *finishing the most important first.*

Putting this into practice can be hard. The truth is that we often don't know what is most important – or what the definition of importance is. You have to begin by understanding the criteria upon which you are going to prioritise. In many ways, understanding what is important is of greater consequence than actually prioritising. If you understand what is important and what is not, your decision making will be easy and fast. If you do not know this, then it will always be difficult.

Typical criteria to judge importance of tasks are financial measures, alignment with strategic goals, or meeting some specific objective of your boss or other stakeholders. Avoid using too few or too many criteria on which you judge importance of activities. Use too many criteria and you will get bogged down in analysis. Too few criteria usually results in overly simplistic decision making. A good place to start looking for criteria is your KPIs (Key Performance Indicators) – but be aware that most businesses expect you to do more than just hit KPIs. Once you develop experience, your intuition will be a great guide.

Decide how prescriptive you need to be in setting priorities for your team. At one extreme is direction setting. Here you give enough information for team members to decide their own priorities. For a small and mature team this is usually enough. At the other extreme, you may need to perform a prescriptive ranking of all activities. In certain high-pressure situations, and for less experienced teams, this may be required.

Ideally, team members develop their abilities to make choices about importance based on your broad guidance. However, if you need to be prescriptive, be prescriptive! Don't roughly bundle things into high, medium or low categories. Make absolutely clear what is top priority and what is bottom priority and what must be stopped. Often just defining what needs to stop is the quickest way to a significantly more efficient team.

Regularly revisit your prioritisations. Don't change priorities all the time or nothing will get done. But revisit priorities at least once a month and amend according to needs. The duration priorities are set for depends on the context. Occasionally, teams need daily priorities set. But for an experienced team monthly direction combined with regular monitoring and feedback to team members should be sufficient.

Test the effectiveness of your prioritisation. One test is to check how clear team members are and how consistent their activities are with your prioritisation. The other is seeing choices being made and activities being stopped. Prioritisation must result in a decision being made, not just the pretence of one. If you spend time prioritising and decide that everything is important, effectively you have made no decision.

It is not the absolute importance of tasks that matters, but the relative importance between the different components of the team's workload. From time to time there will be some important tasks that cannot be done because you have even more important things to do.

Keep the prioritisation process simple. Some managers understand the criticality of prioritising, but make prioritisation an unnecessarily complex science and a time-consuming task. Stay in the real world. Remember that getting things done is more important than the activity of prioritising. Prioritisation should be rapid and straightforward. At first it will be hard, but regular practice will make it brisk and efficient. And don't be afraid of making a prioritisation decision. If you get it wrong, you can easily change it.

The 6 symptoms of poor prioritisation

There is no prioritisation

Managers often struggle with prioritisation. In some organisations there is no attempt to prioritise. Arguments like 'we don't need to prioritise', 'it's too complex' or 'it changes all the time' are made. The form of prioritisation rightly varies – but all organisations need to prioritise.

No one knows what the priorities are

It is essential to thoroughly communicate priorities. Priorities are crucial information to communicate across teams. There is no point going through the effort of prioritising unless everyone is told what the resultant decisions are. Staff cannot work to priorities unless they are clear what they are. As part of the communication of priorities it is important to stress both what is high priority, and what is low priority and should not be worked on.

You don't know what work is ongoing

This is an indirect indication of a lack of prioritisation. To prioritise you must have an understanding of what the possible and actual work is. Therefore if you don't have this picture, even a very high-level perspective, it is unlikely that any prioritisation is taking place.

Everything is high priority

Managers define everything as high priority. A prioritisation process is being undertaken, but it is not effective. The classic example is when a project portfolio is prioritised. Projects are prioritised on a scale of 1 to 3. At the end of the prioritisation 95% of the projects are given priority 1.

This is not prioritisation. It is weak thinking and failure to make decisions. If prioritisation results in all activities having a high priority, then it is not a useful process. Effective prioritisation results in clear decisions *not to undertake* some activities, and in a relatively small selection of high-priority activities to progress.

Personal priorities rule

An absence of explicit prioritisation by managers does not lead to a total lack of prioritisation. In the end, team members have only so many hours in the day and if no prioritisation is indicated, they will prioritise themselves. They have little choice but to do this.

There is nothing intrinsically wrong with delegating prioritisation decisions, but it is at risk from two problems. The first is that unless team members have a well-understood and shared vision of direction, prioritisation decisions taken by different team members will be inconsistent. The second problem follows on from this. Progress will be delayed and resource inefficiently allocated. This happens because of the lack of synchronisation between different individuals.

Conformity with priorities is poor

The final sign of poor prioritisation is that no one conforms to the priorities. Individuals can be surprisingly resistant to priorities they do not like or do not agree with. Team members, especially specialists like project managers, often contribute to this problem. If they are working on a very low priority project, they may see their role as to complete the project irrespective of its priority. Reinforce the point that their job is to deliver projects taking account of the prioritisation, not to ignore priorities.

Work on this more if ...

- You are constantly struggling to deliver your work because of a lack of resources.
- You spend more time arguing about resource allocation than doing productive work.
- Your stakeholders and customers do not agree on how you should allocate your resources.
- You feel you must always try to do everything.
- Usually, priority is given to the work of *he who shouts loudest*, irrespective of business rationale.

Manager's checklist

■ Prioritisation starts by understanding what is important.

■ Don't get overly analytical – it's a tool, not a result in itself.

■ Make prioritisation decisions quickly. If they turn out to be wrong, revisit and amend.

■ Monitor and check for compliance to priorities by team members.

■ Regularly update – but not so frequently that no work gets done.

■ Watch out for the six symptoms of poor prioritisation.

Problems, barriers and conflicts

What is this about and why is it important?

A new manager soon learns that the business world is not perfect and cannot be fully planned. Problems occur that slow down work. Barriers arise which stop the team from progressing. Arguments occur between team members. Some difficulties are predictable and within your power to resolve. Many are unforeseeable and at least partially outside of your control. On top of this, management is concerned with people – and people are neither totally rational nor completely reliable. Conflict will arise.

These problems become interruptions in the flow of the day. In fact, for many managers the working day is about handling interruptions. The only time which is calm and suitable for doing 'real work' is early in the morning or in the evening, when everyone else has gone home.

One phrase that is firmly part of the management vocabulary is *fire fighting* – responding immediately to unexpected issues. Some managers love the cut and thrust of fire fighting. Others hate it.

Given all the other work that managers have to do, such problems are often unwelcome. The best attitude is to embrace them. Solving problems, barriers and conflicts is real work. If nothing ever went wrong, we would not need full-time managers!

Objectives for managers

- To be able to accurately identify and investigate problems facing you or your team.
- To rapidly and effectively resolve the identified problems.
- To focus efforts on problems which you are the right person to resolve.

Common issues in achieving these objectives

- Incomplete understanding leads to a focus on symptoms and not underlying problems.
- Business complexity results in an inability to bound problems into realistically resolvable chunks.
- You are working flat out, and there is no time to sort out unplanned issues.
- There are so many problems that you do not know where to start.

The management guide

The steps in dealing with problems are straightforward:

1. Clarify the problem.
2. Confirm if it is it your problem to resolve.
3. Prioritise.
4. Identify solutions.
5. Resolve and monitor.

Let's look briefly at each one of these steps in turn; having done that we will look at some tips for problem solving.

Clarify the problem

To resolve a problem, you need to know what the problem is. You can waste a lot of effort mitigating symptoms and related issues without fixing real problems. Gaining clarity over problems is essential to effective and efficient resolution. This is especially important when it comes to conflict between team members. Simply clarifying the source of conflict can resolve many such issues.

Make sure you can identify and communicate what the real problem is. When you really understand them, most problems can be explained in a few words. If you are struggling, root cause analysis techniques such as *Five Whys* and *Ishikawa* or *fishbone diagrams* can be helpful.

You not only have to understand the problem, you need to understand the boundaries. Businesses are complex and one aspect leads into another. Processes, systems and teams interrelate. Dig deep enough into an issue and you may find it spreading out across the whole business. If you are not careful and do not limit the scope of a problem you risk trying to re-engineer the whole business. This is impractical and inefficient.

Confirm it is your issue to resolve

Once you understand the problem, check back with yourself – is it really your issue to resolve? Do not get involved in fixing things if it does not add value. It may be better resolved by another manager. If the problem relates to team conflict, sometimes it is necessary to get involved, but on other occasions you have to tell your team members to sort it out themselves. Managers who are too quick to take responsibility for solving problems find all problems coming to their door.

Prioritise

If it is your problem to resolve, how high-priority is it? You have to prioritise this problem into your workload along with all the other things you have to do. In most situations, you do not have the time to do any complex prioritisation. You need a simple, intuitive prioritisation. Such prioritisation should be part of your everyday thinking (see the previous section).

Factors to consider in prioritising problem fixing are: the problem's impact, risk of it getting worse, and how often it occurs. You should also consider whether you can resolve the problem. It sounds obvious on paper, but managers waste a lot of effort trying to fix things they have no control over. If you have no control, work around the problem, don't fix it (see pp. 180–4). Finally, you work in a political world. What is the politics surrounding this issue? Is it important to any senior stakeholders? If it is, prioritise it higher. Managers who do not want to involve themselves in such political considerations are being naive.

Identify solutions

There is no certain technique for identifying solutions to problems. If the problem is well specified and investigated the solution will often be obvious. If it is not, involve your team in solution identification. Creativity is not the preserve of the manager. Brainstorming and other idea-generating techniques can help. There may be expertise somewhere else in the business you can call on. Does anyone else have similar difficulties? What did they do?

Resolve and monitor

Finally, implement the solution to resolve the problem. Monitor to check resolution has worked. It is an unfortunate truth that it will not always be the perfect solution you expect, and some solutions will throw up other problems.

Cross-department and process problems

This is all logical and good, but it does not help resolve one of the biggest issues in business. This is when one department causes a problem, but it is other departments that suffer from it. A classic example of this is when a sales department, in the pressure to hit targets and gain commission, does not write quality orders. The sales team still get their commission so they do not worry about this. The order fulfilment department suffers, having to waste time decoding the forms and chasing up customers for correct information.

One of the solutions to this sort of issue is better process design and cross-process management (rather than purely functional management). This is a great solution, but you cannot re-engineer the business every time you have a difficulty with another department. Resolving this sort of problem, and it is very common, comes down to your ability to negotiate and influence the other department.

In facing this situation, do not start by finger pointing, entering a shouting match, or sending heated emails to the department causing you problems. This will not speed resolution. Make sure you are clear what the problem is and what your ideal solution looks like. Then explain your difficulty and ideal solution to the other department's manager. Try and make it worthwhile for the manager to resolve the problem. Be flexible. There will be situations where this does not work and you need to call on more senior managers. But avoid open warfare. It is very rarely productive.

Other tips in managing problems

Focus on the problems that really do need to be solved and solve them fast. It is not just wishful thinking that some problems will occur only once and will go away. Some may be irritating, but actually are not causing any real performance issue. On the other hand, when you have identified a real problem, don't leave it until it is critical.

Balance being the perfect corporate citizen with doing your own job properly. It's great to be helpful, but solving another team's problems is not always the best thing to do. You should certainly not be doing it when the price is that you do not have time to complete important parts of your own work. There is also a risk in constantly fixing someone else's problems. They have no incentive to ever fix their own issues and never learn how to.

One cause of problems will be disputes between your team members. Sometimes these disputes will spill over into serious conflict that affects productivity. Always remember in such a situation that team members have a duty to act maturely and resolve issues themselves. Before getting involved always challenge the disputants to resolve the issue themselves first. Constantly entering into conflict with other team members, whilst never resolving it without management intervention, should be treated as a serious performance issue.

A contributing factor in such disputes is the use of inappropriate emails. Encourage face-to-face dialogue whenever possible – and if not, the use of a phone. Discourage the use of the cc and bcc email for political reasons, especially when it relates to a one-on-one dispute between team members.

Finally, do not become addicted to fire fighting! We all have to fight fires at times, and when we do then it is great to be good at it. But good management should also be about predicting and avoiding the fires in the first place.

Work on this more if ...

■ Either problems fail to be resolved and are causing an ever-increasing impact on your work, or all you ever do is resolve problems.

Manager's checklist

■ Accept that solving unpredicted problems will always be part of your workload.

■ Start by clarifying and bounding problems.

■ Prioritise and focus on the problems which most benefit the business by being resolved now.

■ Before resolving a problem make sure you are the right person to do it.

■ Negotiate and influence cross-departmental difficulties – avoid warfare!

■ Encourage team members to sort out their own conflicts before escalating to you.

Dealing with change

What is this about and why is it important?

Businesses are under continuous pressure to change. Competitive forces, social adjustments and technology enhancements are some of the pressures driving change. Like it or hate it, you have to learn to deal with change. Ideally managers thrive upon change (although it is always sensible to be a little cynical about those who make this claim for themselves – mostly what they mean is that they thrive on making others change).

In management speak the word *change* covers a lot of different activities. Change encompasses everything from incremental improvements to the largest radical programmes. There are systems implementations, reorganisations, restructuring, process redesigns, cultural transformation – all of these are change. There are also change aspects to activities like launching new products, relocations, business expansions as well as mergers and acquisitions.

Change is not an occasional event, but is an ongoing part of a manager's workload. Being able to deal with change is not an advanced skill that you can wait to develop when you have significant experience. It is a basic skill that all managers need to have some competency in.

Change management skills are important for your career development. Few jobs are assessed purely on day-to-day performance. Assessments take account of change management capabilities. This includes your ability to deliver continuous performance improvements as well as supporting large change initiatives in a business. Change skills are included in many management job specifications.

Objectives for managers

- To be able to support the business by implementing change in your team effectively.
- To assist your team going through regular changes.
- To be able to deliver your own improvements within your team.
- To survive change personally!

Common issues in achieving these objectives

- Change creates an extra, unsustainable, workload for managers and their teams.
- Team members resist changes.
- Change risks operational disruptions, causing performance targets to be missed.
- Change is not maintained after a change initiative is complete.

The management guide

There are many varieties of change initiative, but there are essentially two situations you need to deal with:

- You are the originator of change. Unless you are in a senior position this will probably be small incremental changes within your own team.
- Changes imposed on you and your team. These will be a regular occurrence for most teams, and from time to time will be profound.

There is an image of change being implemented by the visionary senior manager or by a hard-working change team. These may be necessary, but are not sufficient to deliver change. The point that is rarely stated is that change is not implemented by project teams or change sponsors. Change is implemented by managers working with their teams. You and all your management peers are the change team. If you and your peers do not actively pursue the change, it will not happen.

Let's look briefly at some key aspects of change for a manager.

Create a team environment which enables change

Change works best if your team has an environment which enables change. Creating the right environment is an ongoing part of management, rather than part of a specific change initiative. The aim is to have a team that responds positively to change. Important aspects of this are:

■ Regularly setting the expectation that things will change and will continue to change.

■ Explicitly encouraging and rewarding behaviour which is consistent with change.

■ Supporting continuous innovation and improvement in the ways of working.

■ Giving your team members familiarity with change. Ideally, enable team members to become involved in change projects – not just for your team, but across the business.

■ Limiting feelings of entitlement. Your team members have many valid entitlements, but do not let entitlements proliferate – this just makes change harder.

Help individuals in your team through changes

We talk about businesses, divisions and teams changing. This language places emphasis on the change at a group level. This is critically important for a business, and its success in delivering change is a result of modifications of groups. But the problem with this language is that we can lose sight of the individual. In the end, change is a result of the cumulative modifications in behaviour of the individuals in an organisation. Change happens at the individual level.

With regard to your team, you should ensure that each member:

- Understands the change and what it means for their role.
- Is capable of working in the changed way. This may require coaching, education or training.
- Is willing to work in the changed way.
- Is motivated to continue to work in the changed way, and does not revert to previous ways of working when the focus is no longer on this change.

A major component of change management is concerned with dealing with resistance. One of your key roles will be assessing and dealing with this resistance.

Change is made by people. It is not made by new systems, processes or tools. Change may require modified systems, processes and tools, but it is people's adoption of them that is the change. Implementing change is simply getting people to work in a modified fashion. People experience change personally. If no one experiences it personally, nothing has changed! There is a standard human response to change: resistance. Resistance occurs for a range of practical and psychological reasons. The level of response depends on the individual and their interpretation of and perceived relationship to the change.

Resistance is an inevitable part of change. If there is no resistance then there is no belief that the change will occur. You should not underestimate it, nor should you assume it will be immediately apparent. You can assess and prepare for resistance and attempt to reduce it, but you cannot eliminate it – and it is not your enemy. It is just a fact of life that must be managed.

Ensure the team keeps delivering

One common outcome from a change initiative is a reduction in performance. Sometimes this is inevitable and unavoidable, but often it is simply a result of not focusing on normal work in the excitement or pressure of the change initiative. There are often valid reasons for drops in performance, but you will not get any credit. You cannot take your eye off the day job during change.

To ensure there is minimal disruption of your team's performance during change:

■ Keep team members focused on team goals. Change can undermine all of the hard work you have put into making goals shared and clear. There is a risk that during change people can start working to their own agendas. A key aspect of change management is therefore keeping people focused on the real work of the department.

■ Ensure deliverables from change programmes are fit for purpose and will enable you to achieve your performance targets.

■ Try to influence initiative sponsors to implement changes at the most appropriate times. This means avoiding times of peak workload and trying to slot changes in when you are less busy.

■ Manage the expectations of your key stakeholders up front if performance reductions are unavoidable or likely.

Sustain change

Change initiatives come to an end. Management attention moves on to the next thing. The current change is no longer central. Unless an organisation is careful, change can unravel when an initiative ends. To prevent this:

■ Avoid ending change initiatives until the change is the normal way of working and is fully embedded.

■ Ensure your own behaviour is aligned with change outcomes. If you are not working with the change, your team won't either. Even small gaps between your behaviour and the desired change will be noticed.

■ Continue to encourage adherence to change outcomes explicitly.

■ Listen to team members. Help them to deal with their issues, and to feed back valid concerns and problems to the initiative before it ends.

Help yourself

Times of change can be challenging for a manager. The workload can be intense. You have your personal responses to the change to deal with. You may have split loyalties. You are an agent of the firm ensuring that the necessary change occurs. You are also a member of the team, personally impacted by a change.

We can all handle some levels of stress. If you get very stressed every time change comes along, then management is probably not the place for you. However, if you are early in your career then undoubtedly the first time you implement significant change will be stressful. This is normal. It will get easier! Two tips:

- Try and always keep some capacity to deal with change, both in yourself and within the team. If you are flat out doing the day job then change will be difficult.
- Try to be flexible and open to change. Do not start to consider anything at work as immutable. All aspects of a business can, and probably will, change. Be ready for this.

For your own career good, don't respond passively to change. Often, you will have opportunity to influence a change, especially if you get involved in the early stages. Think about the initiative's implication for your own role, and work out practical courses of action – in advance.

If you are really not in a good position, work out what you are going to do. If your role will disappear as part of a change, do your job professionally and start lining up a new role. Don't panic – businesses always need managers who can implement change.

Work on this more if ...

- Change regularly creates significant disruption to working relationships or performance.
- Change never sticks in your team.
- You find times of change overly demanding or stressful.

Manager's checklist

■ Create an environment in which your team is able to adapt to changes.

■ Help individuals through the change.

■ Ensure the team keeps delivering whilst change is ongoing.

■ Work to sustain changes after change initiatives are complete.

■ Help yourself through the change. Prepare personally for the outcome – in advance.

seven

The sophisticated manager

Each manager has a personal opinion about the constituents of management, and approaches the tasks of management with a specific level of sophistication. Every manager performs activities such as recruiting team members, delegating activity and doing performance reviews.

Your success as a manager is partially a result of how well you undertake these common tasks. But it is also a function of how sophisticated your concept of management is. This part explores four areas where sophisticated managers can distinguish themselves through an enhanced view of management.

The first section challenges the myth of certainty in management and the flimsiness of much that is defined as best practice, and looks at the implications for your work.

The second section explores risk taking for managers, and how it can be advantageous for you to take risks. Risk taking is not only beneficial for businesses, it can help your career.

There are many other sources of valuable ideas outside of the conventional management body of knowledge. The third section provides an example of one set of thinking which did not originate in management, but can provide inspiration for managers.

The last section of this part considers language. What you say and how you say it differentiates you as a manager probably more than any other factor. Yet it is comparatively rare for managers to think about their use of language.

The myths of management science and predictable futures

What is this about and why is it important?

Let's look at the context of modern management.

For decades management tools and techniques have been studied and developed. Intuition and gut feel have been surpassed. A standard model of management has arisen, based on the belief that management is a science resulting in predictable outcomes if the right approach is followed.

Managers learn how to manage from their own experiences and from the collected wisdom of other managers and commentators. This experience is collated and labelled as *best practice*. Sometimes this best practice is formalised into training courses – from short events through to MBAs.

Good managers make a variety of predictions against the future. These predictions are based on models of how the world operates. The manager aims to achieve best practice in some area or another. She predicts how this will be achieved, what budget is required, and the plans for achieving it. The predictions are documented in business cases, project plans, forecasts, financial models and budgets. These describe what is expected to happen in future. Having made such a prediction, it becomes a commitment the manager's performance will be judged against.

It is accepted that we do not know everything, so predictions are based on documented assumptions. It is also accepted that there is a degree of unpredictability, so risks are identified.

The culture of business values detailed predictions above broad-brush estimates. Businesses value managers whose results or *actuals* match their predictions. This is reinforced by the press, commentators and stock markets. If you cannot predict accurately, surely that means you do not know what you are doing?

You have to work within this culture and using these models. This section explores the flaws in them.

Objectives for managers

- To understand the strengths and limitations of management predictions, forecasts, budgets and plans.
- To be able to make predictions about the future, whilst understanding the weaknesses of these predictions.

Common issues in achieving these objectives

- Generalisations are confused with universal laws.
- Inability to predict accurately is perceived as incompetence.

The management guide

Flaws in the standard model

There are several fundamental flaws in the standard model. They are not hard to identify, and deep down everyone in business knows them. The flaws are clearly expressed by those who are new to business – asking questions like *why on earth do we do it like that?*

The most obvious problems are that there is always too limited information to make an accurate prediction. On top of this the world changes and so the conditions at the time of the prediction are not the same as those at the time of the result. We have limited foresight. This is why forecasts make risks and assumptions explicit, and if they are sophisticated, provide some form of sensitivity analysis.

The problem of limited information is real, but also generally understood. There are more insidious problems deriving from the status of management laws and the behaviour of managers.

Management is not a fully understood science whose pronouncements have the validity of laws of nature. It is at best a series of reasonably consistent empirical viewpoints based on limited samples of data. The rules and algorithms are mostly rough estimates and rules of thumb. Management forecasts usually concern the behaviour of people, and assume people are rational. There is plenty of evidence that human beings are not. There is nothing wrong with this as long as the limitations of management models are always borne in mind. All too often, they arc not.

Underlying this is a confusion between broad generalisations and universal laws. When an action results in an outcome it is assumed that this is repeatable – this inductive logic is the basis of science. But it is only repeatable if the conditions are the same. Conditions are never exactly the same and it is not clear what makes conditions sufficiently similar for an action to result predictably in the same outcome. Rather than doubt the generalisation, it is assumed that conditions are similar enough – and best practice is developed, which is treated as if it is a law. This can be seen in the tendency in business to go from 'I have observed' to 'it is true that' to 'you should' to 'everyone must' without the requisite additional evidence.

Another issue is management behaviour. I am not suggesting that all managers behave as I am about to describe – but some, and often many, do.

Managers are not stupid. Managers know that understandings are incomplete and therefore they build safety factors into predictions. Often huge safety factors which overestimate needs, at least if the manager can get away with it. This results in the normal budgeting game where managers ask for as much as they can, and their line managers challenge them and try to reduce it as much as possible. Neither side really knows what is required – but the assumption is that if the manager is challenged enough, the resulting compromise will be right. If a manager gains a larger budget than required, the aim is to achieve expected results using up the entire budget. Hence the actuals will match predictions.

Managers use the process of prediction not to find answers but to justify an approach. Managers know the answer needed from a prediction to justify their approach. Inputs, algorithms and assumptions are fudged to produce the answer desired.

Some managers actually don't care about predicted results. If the manager is making a prediction several years into the future, she knows her tenure in role will be shorter than this. She has no reason to worry if the prediction is right or wrong. It is just a mechanism to gain approval. The first thing a new manager taking over the role will do is to reset the baseline of all the major plans and forecasts and blame any problems on her predecessor.

Flaws in the objectives

Even if the management models are flawed, surely what they are trying to achieve is right? If we continue to collect evidence and build better models won't this solve the problem? It may help, but it will not solve the underlying problem. The problem is not just the way the standard model achieves its objectives. The problem is that the objectives are flawed. The objectives are:

- To have perfect predictability.
- To replace subjectivity and intuition with universal best practice and science.

Perfect predictability is a myth, an unobtainable goal. Anyway, shouldn't managers be aiming for the best result, rather than the most predictable?

Many successful entrepreneurs rely on intuition. They tend to smirk at management models and calculations. Intuition is fast and uses very limited resources in coming to decisions and insights. Modelling, forecasting and predictions use up huge amount of resources, without actually delivering anything of real value. A business makes no product, sells nothing and satisfies no customer by forecasting.

You don't want better algorithms and even more data. You want better intuition. The reason managers avoid intuition is because it does not fit in the way organisations work. No one gains a budget because they convince their manager that they have an intuition.

The problem with universal best practice is that it goes against all needs of competitive business. If you apply the same best practice as your competitors you will be the same as them. When someone does something better you will be uncompetitive or may go out of business. And although *best* practice implies there should not be something better, sooner or later there will be.

Why bother?

The conclusion from this may seem to be, why should I bother to make predictions? There are good reasons why you should bother.

The first is that forecasting, planning and budgeting are part of the ritual of business. Every society has its own rituals and customs, and if you want to be part of it you need to conform. You can argue all you like about the flaws in budgets and forecasts, but if you don't play along you won't be in the business for long. As much as anything planning, budgeting and forecasting processes are political processes. You will be judged not simply for your results, but for how well you act the expected role of a manager in performing these activities. If you do not perform, you will get nowhere.

Secondly, flawed is not the same as being of no use. I have been very critical, but good forecasts and plans, used appropriately, are powerful. Although it may be rare, there are some situations in which you understand the conditions well, and your level of accuracy in a forecast will be high. But even more generally, forecasts, plans and predictions are useful, as long as:

- You use them as guides, not answers.
- You understand the degree of accuracy and sensitivities in them.
- You are aware of the risks and assumptions made in the model, and if these turn out to materialise, then you do something about it.

- You invest a proportionate amount of time in developing forecasts. Ideally, this is a relatively small proportion of your overall time.

Finally, as general guidance, be cynical about anything labelled *best practice*. It may or may not be. If you are presented with best practice, ask who defined it as best practice, based on what sample of data.

Work on this more if ...

- You are concerned or stressed about your ability to forecast and plan.
- You think forecasting and planning are a waste of time and want to stop doing them.
- You spend a significant proportion of your time forecasting (unless you are a professional forecaster).

Manager's checklist

- The standard model of predictable outcomes in business is flawed.
- Management is not (yet?) a science.
- However, you have to make predictions, plans, budgets and forecasts as this is the norm in business and you are not in a position to change it.
- You should forecast, predict and plan as they are useful and powerful activities. But use them with your eyes open, understanding their inherent flaws.

Taking risks as a manager

What is this about and why is it important?

Risk is a feature of management. The future is uncertain, information is imperfect, and cognitive abilities are limited. Various techniques for handling risk exist, labelled as *risk management*.

This section looks at the risks that derive from being a manager. In most management roles, risk management does not need to be complex or sophisticated. You need an intuitive sense for risk and a practical approach to handling it. (It is beyond the scope of this book to provide a detailed treatise on risk management or to discuss the risks deriving from your business.)

Risk management techniques revolve around identifying potential risks and then deciding what to do about them. Some risks you can live with. Some can be avoided or at least reduced in likelihood of occurring. Other risks should be prepared for, just in case they are realised. You cannot remove risk completely. You have to deal with it one way or another.

Risk is a problem that has to be borne, but it is also an opportunity you can take advantage of. There can be significant rewards for taking risk, at least for taking risks that pay off. One way of differentiating yourself from your peers is in the way you choose which risks to take and how successful you are in dealing with them.

Objectives for managers

- To develop an intuitive sense for identifying risk.
- To learn a pragmatic approach to dealing with risk.
- Where you have a choice, to choose the right risks to take.

Common issues in achieving these objectives

- A tendency to ignore risk and assume predictions and plans are foolproof.

- Wrong balance in risk management. Too much analysis and too little or too slow action in dealing with common risks, contrasted with a lack of sufficient analysis of the few big risks that require it.

- Risk-averse personality and management culture reduces the propensity to take risks with acceptable probabilities of good pay-offs.

The management guide

There is a simple model of risk. This model has limitations, but is sufficient for most uses. If you need something sophisticated get trained in or read up on specialist risk management techniques. In this model risks have two independent dimensions: likelihood and impact. *Likelihood* refers to the probability a risk will occur. *Impact* refers to the effect should the risk occur. The most benign risks have low likelihood and low impact, and the most worrying risks have high likelihood and high impact.

Categories of risk

There are three categories of risk for managers:

1. The risks inherent in your job. These are the risks that cannot be avoided. You have to work with them.

2. Small risks, which can be avoided, but which you can choose as they may benefit you or your team.

3. Big optional risks. You can avoid these. They are potentially disastrous if you get them wrong, but get them right and the pay-off can be high.

Let's look at some examples of each of these.

Most of the risks inherent in your job have a low impact, although many have a fairly high likelihood of occurring. Whilst you may find more of these risks in a management role, to some extent these go with any job. Examples of the risks inherent in your job are:

- Making poor decisions on a daily basis in the absence of sufficient information. Often you will have to balance the time to research and think against the need to make decisions quickly.
- Selecting the wrong priorities. This means focusing on the wrong activities, and choosing to ignore the activities you should be doing.
- Making a mistake. Instances include leaving something inadvertently out of your team's work schedule or choosing a sub-optimal solution to a problem.

The second category of risk is directly related to your role as a manager. As a manager you face choices on a daily basis. Sometimes you have the option of a low-risk solution, but for various reasons you may choose a higher-risk solution. In most cases, the impact of your choice going wrong is acceptable – at worst you may get a slapped wrist from your boss. Instances of these risks are:

- Allocating work to an inexperienced team member when you also have the choice of a reliably experienced expert (see pp. 89–94).
- Taking short cuts with agreed processes such as budgeting or talent management. You choose not to prioritise the activity highly enough and do not allocate the time to fulfil it.
- Sharing politically sensitive information with a colleague you do not fully trust.

Beyond this are the truly optional risks. Some managers never take any risk of this sort in their whole careers. Others, typically those who are more ambitious, self-confident or unwise, do. The frequency of these options is low. The impact of it going wrong to you personally is high. Examples include:

- Choosing to take on a challenging project several people have failed at before.

- Saying yes to an important stakeholder, when you do not understand what he is asking for or how you will do it – but politically it seems the right thing to do (see pp. 58–61).
- Performing a critical task contrary to the habit or cultural norm of the organisation, or against the desire of a powerful stakeholder.

Dealing with risk – generally

When it comes to risk, you are not alone. Risk is inherent in your work. You cannot remove it, but it is not only you who have to deal with it. Everyone doing your sort of job is facing the same sort of challenges. However, if you are observant and sensible you can avoid the worst risks unless you choose to take them.

Do not worry about most of the everyday risks you face. It is the cumulative profile of risks and the average outcome that matters, not the individual risks. Think of your choices in terms of a portfolio. As long as you get most choices right, and avoid getting the important ones wrong, the small ones you get wrong or sub-optimal will be lost, ignored and hidden in the portfolio average.

Be aware of risk, make assessments, but do not spend too much time on analysis. If a lack of information is a source of risk, it is also a limitation on your ability to process and assess risk. When information is scarce there is little point in trying to perform complex analysis or execute resource-intensive algorithms. The assumptions you make will be as risky as the risk itself.

Reduce your risk by sharing it. If you feel overwhelmed by a risk, talk to your boss. Get his insight as to how to overcome it, and his approval of your way forward. Once this has happened you are not standing alone – the risk is now your boss's. It is in your boss's interest for you to get as much right as possible. However, don't share risk with him all the time as it is irritating for your boss, and shows you are incapable of making judgements and decisions.

Dealing with each category of risk

With the first category of risk, do not over-analyse. Quickly assess the situation and make the choice that seems right. If you are unsure, try something out. Learn as your experience grows. Pick out the few choices that are more significant and take more care in your decision making. Get used to this type of risk.

Treat the second category of risk similarly to the first. Do not take on every single risk of this type, but even though these are optional, you need to take some of these risks. In the short run you take some hazard, in the longer run you will tend to decrease risk and improve performance. For example, if you never allocate work to the inexperienced team members, they will never learn and you will limit your capacity as a team. If you let them learn, you increase capacity and make yourself more flexible for those times when there is no choice but to allocate work to them. Over time you will naturally get better at assessing and taking these sorts of risk. As long as you get most of them right, or at least not obviously wrong, then you will be fine.

With the third category of risk, you have a choice. Sooner or later you will come across them. If you want to avoid them, then usually you can sidestep them. But if you want to excel in your career you need to take risks like these. Choose with care, and try to stick with things you have some familiarity with or a different approach to. The nightmare project no one else wants to touch may really be a poisoned chalice that must be avoided. On the other hand, it may just seem such and if you approach it in a different way you will overcome it. Overcoming a problem that others saw as impossible will help your career.

Do not become over bullish about taking on risk. No one ever gets penalised for quietly shelving or avoiding promising but risky ideas. On the other hand, if you pursue a risky idea and it fails, you will be penalised. Yet real success comes about by taking risks and distinguishing the business and yourself. A career can be built on a few big things pulled off well.

Options

Most decision making is about choosing and removing options. But the future is uncertain, and no matter how much information you have, your choice may be sub-optimal. If you wait a while before making a decision it may improve as the information you have improves. However, sometimes you are best off making a choice and sticking with it.

An alternative approach is to keep your options open. There can be significant value in keeping your options open. Financial services have built a whole industry on the value of options. Sometimes rather than choosing A over B, it is better to invest a little more time and resource progressing both A and B – not because the final outcome makes it worth doing both A and B, but because there is value in continuing to have the option of doing A and B.

Whenever you are making a choice between options, especially if the decision is significant and irreversible, ask yourself whether you really have to make a choice now. There is a balance to be found between rapid decision making and commitment, and remaining flexible. Successful businesses are nimble, making decisions quickly and focusing on a limited range of activities. But successful businesses are also flexible, keeping their options open where appropriate.

Work on this more if ...

- You are confused and cannot make decisions in the face of risk.
- You are stressed or uncomfortable with the everyday risks you face as a manager.
- You are ambitious and want to differentiate yourself from your peers by doing something big and bold.

Manager's checklist

- There are everyday risks you cannot avoid. Make a decision and learn from the consequences.

- There are optional short-term risks you can take which will reduce longer-term risk. You must pursue some of these.

- There are big optional risks. You have a choice over these. Choose carefully, but if you are ambitious sooner or later you should take one.

- Options have a value. Keeping your options open may be worthwhile.

Learning from the Stoics

What is this about and why is it important?

Managers learn from their personal experiences of work and from other managers in business. Yet when you think about the task of management it is apparent that many aspects of it are not unique to business. Activities such as running teams, interacting and influencing people, overcoming problems or synthesising complex information are fundamental to successful management, but are also required in many other parts of life.

There has been a trend in business to read certain non-management books, and try to apply the lessons to business. Classic examples are Sun Tzu's *The Art of War*, Machiavelli's *The Prince* or seemingly any book with the story of a great sporting champion. Some of the choices work better than others. I have chosen a less common and very different example of a stream of thinking which I think has many useful thoughts for managers: stoicism.

Stoicism was a school of philosophy in ancient Greece and classical Rome. When we talk of 'stoical' behaviour nowadays we refer to someone who can put up with discomfort or pain without complaining. Stoics would support this behaviour, but they had a much wider range of beliefs. Some of these beliefs may seem bizarre or incomprehensible to us now, but others are interesting and many aspects of their thought are appealing.

Famous Stoics included Zeno of Citium, Cleanthes, Chrysippus, Epictetus and Seneca. In this section all the quotes are from probably the most famous stoical writer and his celebrated book, the Roman emperor Marcus Aurelius and his book called *Meditations*. I have chosen five short quotations to help you to think about your management attitudes and behaviours, and to encourage you to read more.

It is sometimes hard to determine exactly what ancient philosophers meant by their statements in their time. But we can apply the words in our context and in doing so we find that there are many lessons for us. Read this section for the thoughts of the Stoics, and to open your mind to the extensive body of knowledge which is applicable to management.

Objectives for managers

■ To see an example of a different source of helpful management thinking.

■ To open your horizons to wider perspectives which can help with management.

Common issues in achieving these objectives

■ Unwillingness to explore alternative sources of management insight.

■ Inappropriate examples being used as metaphors for business, which put people off seeking external ideas.

The management guide

Selected lessons from *Meditations*

Because a thing is difficult for you, do not therefore suppose it to be beyond mortal power. On the contrary, if anything is possible and proper for a man to do, assume that it must fall within your own capacity.

(*Meditations*, Book 6, 19)

To pursue the unattainable is insanity, yet the thoughtless can never refrain from doing it.

(*Meditations*, Book 5, 17)

I have started with two quotes which summarise the balance you need to find at work. On one hand, you should seek out demanding challenges and not avoid tasks because they are hard. On the other, you need to maintain a sense of realism and avoid wasting time on the impractical.

Positive thinking is extremely powerful. People who think positively tend to be happier and healthier. Managers who think positively achieve far more than those who don't. When you think positively challenges which initially appear impossible can become possible. And if something is possible, it may well be possible for you. Never accept that something cannot be done simply because no one has managed to do it so far.

But the naive belief that you can do everything, just because you believe you can, is destructive. Unless positive thinking is associated with competence and hard work you will be disappointed. You can almost certainly do far more than you currently now imagine, but no one can do everything.

There are some goals you and your team will never achieve. They are beyond your management abilities, resources or influence. Such goals are a waste of time striving for.

There are many things in most organisations that irritate us and seem sub-optimal. Everyone finds themselves sometimes asking at work *why on earth do we do it like that*? When you find yourself thinking like this: challenge yourself, do not take things for granted, and do not put up with the answer *it's just the way things are*. But there is no point worrying about or trying to alter something beyond your abilities, resources or influence.

When you are the CEO or CFO you may productively question the way forecasting or budgeting is done, for example. But in your first management role you have no ability to influence these sorts of things. So, learn to live with them, and taking another lesson from the Stoics, what you cannot influence, learn to accept with equanimity.

I have seen many managers wasting huge amounts of effort, and developing unnecessary stress trying to change things that are outside of their reach. On the other hand, I have often seen managers overcoming challenges that their peers and associates thought to be impossible. Be ambitious, but don't waste your time.

Loss is nothing else but change, and change is Nature's delight.

(*Meditations*, Book 9, 35)

If you want to survive in business, you must accept that change is inevitable and embrace it. You cannot stop the progress of technology, the innovations of competitors, or the evolution of social attitudes. The most central, stable and critical parts of your business are always vulnerable to transformations you have not thought about and cannot yet envisage.

Everyone is comfortable with the familiar. Modifications to products, services or ways of working can cause a sense of loss. As a manager, you must never expect that the nature of the role you are doing now will be the same for the whole of your career. Don't fight against change, prepare for it. Be open to new ideas.

To be of value and sought after as a manager in the short term you must have current skills that are useful to business. To be of value and sought after as a manager in the long term you must have the ability and willingness to adapt and enhance your skills.

If a man makes a slip, admonish him gently and show him his mistake. If you fail to convince him, blame yourself.

(*Meditations*, Book 10, 4)

As a manager you are responsible for your team's performance. In many cases you selected the members of your team. From time to time team members will make mistakes. It is your role to help your team to develop, and when a team member fails it is not just a problem it is also a learning opportunity.

Focus your instruction or coaching on the mistake and not on penalising the person. If a team member does not develop, arguably it is you who has failed, because you either chose the wrong person for the team or failed to help them develop.

Manifestly, no condition of life could be so well adapted for the practice of philosophy as this in which chance finds you today!

(*Meditations*, Book 11, 7)

You can constantly wait for the perfect conditions to pursue your philosophy, your goals or your management aspirations. But the only time you ever have is today. Today is always the best opportunity you have.

Beyond the Stoics

There are some particular aspects of management that you will only learn by being a manager. But most of these are industry-specific activities. Many of the core skills of being a manager are not unique to management and there is much to learn from other sources.

Stoicism is one example of the vast body of ideas that can be helpful. If Stoicism is not specifically appealing to you, there are millions of other sources out there. By opening your eyes to alternative perspectives you can find inspiration and ideas that will help your management skills develop.

Work on this more if ...

■ You feel the need for alternative sources of inspiration or help in enhancing your own management development.

■ You want to find unconventional or novel ways of presenting ideas to help your team develop.

Manager's checklist

■ Many activities that managers do are not unique to management. Therefore the standard management sources of information are not the only places to seek ideas for improvement.

■ The Stoics had many ideas which can still be easily found and read, and which are insightful even in the modern age.

Language as a tool

What is this about and why is it important?

The most important management tool that you use every day in every situation is one you probably give little thought to: language. Language is fundamental to achieving your goals and aspirations as a manager. Communication is the lifeblood that enables an organisation to exist and thrive.

Language is essential to giving instructions, negotiating, collecting and sharing information, interviewing and persuading. This list could be extended to everything you do as a manager. Management is concerned with influencing people. The tool for influencing is language.

Communication is a goal-directed activity. It is done for a reason, and depending on how effectively you use language you are more or less likely to achieve your goals. But language does more than this, it is central to building relationships. Relationships are profoundly affected by what and how you communicate. To a large extent the relationships you build are a result of your communication.

On top of this, you are constantly assessed by what and how you talk. People judge others by the way they communicate. The more proficient you are in the use of language, the easier you will find your job and the more likely you are to be promoted. Everyone can improve their communication skills.

Objectives for managers

■ To understand the critical importance of language to managers.

■ To develop the best management communication skills that you can.

Common issues in achieving these objectives

- Lack of awareness of language and communication skills.
- Taking language for granted and not thinking about its criticality.

The management guide

Ten ground rules for good communication

As a manager you should always try to communicate clearly and concisely. Management communication is not concerned primarily with perfect oratory or the pleasure of words. It is fantastic if you are brilliant with words, but this is not essential. Management communication is functional. As such the words and information contained should be correct, to the point, and informative for the audience you are communicating to. But to be effective language also needs to be engaging.

The table here contains ten general ground rules for management communication.

	Ground rule	Comments
1	**Before you communicate anything understand what you are trying to achieve**	Why are you communicating? If you cannot answer this question, you will never communicate coherently. The main reason so much management talk is incoherent is that the speakers do not understand clearly enough why they are talking. A vague feeling that *I need to communicate* is not sufficient. If you are going to open your mouth it should be for a reason. Understand this reason and design your communication to fulfil it.
2	**Tailor communication to the audience**	Various groups respond to different language, formats, media, timing etc. You have many audiences and there is rarely a single best form of communication. If you say the same thing in the same way to everyone, you will not communicate effectively.
		There are many media formats and channels for communicating. Do not become fixated on one or another (such as only using PowerPoint presentations). Flex to the situation and the audience.

3 **Make communication as intimate and personally relevant as possible**	The less personally relevant the communication is to the audience, the less effective it tends to be. Of course, you cannot talk individually to everyone about everything. Some things have to be emailed to everyone, but it is never as effective as a one-to-one interaction tailored to the individual. A balance must be found, and in general taking the effort to find time to talk to and listen to smaller groups pays dividends.
4 **Regularly repeat your communications**	You will rarely be heard or fully understood the first time you say something, especially if the audience is large, the content is complex, or the message is contentious or unwelcome.
5 **Be consistent in what you say**	Repetition works best if you are consistent in what you say. Of course, messages evolve, but if you are inconsistent you will cause confusion and lose trust. You may also look incompetent.
6 **Align your behaviour and actions with your words**	Consistency is not just about saying the same thing again and again. You communicate far more than what you say. You communicate by what you are seen to do and how you do it. If your actions do not match your words people will notice – and it is your actions they will follow.
7 **Don't communicate for the sake of it, but don't let a vacuum arise**	You can waste time and effort on bad communication. People hate vacuous talk without substance. It wastes everyone's time. But teams expect their managers to communicate regularly with them. Not talking at all leaves a vacuum which is filled with rumour and gossip. This is rarely helpful.
8 **Listen much more than you speak**	Understanding comes from listening. Communication is a two-way process. Listening enables you to gather information and understand responses to your ideas. Listening also shows respect and builds relationships and trust. If people feel they are never listened to, they have a tendency to stop listening. The way you respond when you listen can encourage or inhibit communication from your team. Have the attitude that every opinion is welcome, never 'shoot the messenger' and you will find out all sorts of useful information. If you constantly respond negatively to team members' comments and questions you will find they stop speaking to you.
9 **Plan your key communications**	Critical communications should be planned. If not, they may seem unprofessional by being inconsistent and insufficient. However, having a plan must not stop you being spontaneous when required.

Ground rule	Comments
10 **Don't mistake talking for making progress.**	Communication is an important tool. It is not the result.

(Adapted from *Financial Times Briefings: Change Management*, Financial Times Prentice Hall © Richard Newton, 2011)

The problems with words

In communicating you assume that the other party is a competent speaker who has a sufficiently similar understanding of words to yours. Their understanding does not have to be exactly the same as yours, but the greater the difference in the meanings individuals apply to words, the greater the communication gap.

There are two risks with this assumption:

1. Your listener's understanding may not be sufficiently similar. Many business words are not ones that are used in private life or in society as a whole. Or if they are, they are used in a different way. Individuals' understanding of even common business terms like *plan* or *change management* varies, and depends on how they have understood the words to be applied before. This can be context specific and wildly different from your meaning.

2. Your listener may not be a competent speaker. Rather than misunderstand your words, a listener may not understand them at all. In a business context, surrounded by judgemental peers and senior managers, it can often be too embarrassing to admit to not understanding a word.

How do you avoid these problems?

The starting point for clear communication is to use simple words. Academics use words precisely, but they often use unfamiliar words and long sentences. Hence academics' books are not popular outside academic circles. The most popular management writers and speakers use simple words and short sentences.

When you are communicating always invite questions. Then it is more likely that your listeners will ask for the meaning of words if they do not understand. Rather than thinking them foolish for not knowing, think of them as wise for asking. If you cannot define the words you are using, you will look the fool! The converse applies to you. You should never be afraid to ask for words to be defined. If the speaker cannot define the word, then doubt their competency to use it.

Regularly define words, even common ones, if there is a risk of misunderstanding. Take a word like *strategy*. This is an important word that is used regularly in business. But I am certain that if you took a random sample of a dozen managers and asked them to define *strategy* they would come up with different meanings. This is hardly the basis for effective communications.

Finally, avoid fads for using novel words just for the sake of it. Whatever you may think, it is never clever in a business context to use an unfamiliar word for a familiar concept. If you have a new concept, which the existing management vocabulary does not encompass, then use a new or different word, but define it whenever you use it.

Beyond language

I have focused on language in this section, but it is always important to remember communication is not just about the words you use. It is impacted by a whole host of other factors.

People are constantly interpreting others: words, behaviour, looks and body language. A man just has to walk into a room, and rightly or wrongly, how he is dressed, what he looks like, his body language and facial gestures and whatever behaviour he exhibits will be interpreted by you. In turn, you communicate all the time, whether deliberately or not and whether you are speaking or not. You are constantly being assessed.

Do not be paranoid, but do be conscious. From time to time it is worth asking for feedback on how people perceive you. It can be very enlightening. Techniques such as NLP (neuro-linguistic programming) can make you significantly more aware of your body language and how to use it effectively.

Work on this more if ...

- Your communication does not achieve the results you expect it to.
- You have had feedback that you need to improve your communication skills.

Manager's checklist

- Communication and the way you use language are essential to achieving your goals as a manager and to building relationships. They are also a critical influence on how you are judged.

- It helps to be a great speaker or writer, but it is not essential for management success. However, you must be able to communicate clearly.

- Take care with the words you use. Many common management words do not have fixed definitions, and management culture is such that it can be difficult to ask for meanings in some situations. Use simple, clear words wherever possible.

- Communication is built on words, but not only words. Whatever you do or don't do will be interpreted constantly by those around you. You assess others and are being assessed all the time.

part

eight

The complete manager

This book has focused, so far, on the essential aspect of management: the role of managers running teams within businesses. But the role of a manager is broader than just these core aspects. This part fills out your picture of management further.

The first section of this part will help you to understand what being a good manager means. You will struggle to be a good manager if you do not have a clear view of what being good means.

A short book of this scale cannot encompass the full diversity of all management roles. The second section summarises additional tasks you typically need to do as a manager and therefore need to be competent at.

In pursing your management career it can be easy to become focused on goals and to lose sight of the fundamentals of ethical behaviour. At times, ethics and a thriving business can seem to be in conflict. They do not need to be. The third section considers how you can combine a successful career as a manager with ethical behaviour.

The final section ends this part by describing the approach you should take to excel in your career – excelling being defined in terms of both doing as good a job as you are capable of and achieving career progression.

What is a good job as a manager?

What is this about and why is it important?

The role of a manager can be confusing. Some days it seems clear and certain what is required; at other times it can feel so indeterminate and volatile that you have no sight of your goals. As you become more experienced these feelings will decline. But even experienced managers can sometimes feel unsure or be mistaken in where they think they should focus their efforts.

It is worth periodically reflecting on what 'good' means when it comes to judging the job you are performing.

Objectives for managers

- To have a clear understanding of what a good job as a manager is.
- To be able to focus on the most value-adding activities of a manager.

Common issues in achieving these objectives

- Having too many possible tasks leads to confusion.
- Tendency to focus on the most urgent tasks rather than the most important.
- Perfectionists who never let go until a perfect result is achieved.
- Trying to do a little of everything.
- Blinkered management only focusing on what is directly in sight.

The management guide

The nature of a good job in management

What is judged to be a good job as a manager is context- and time-specific. There is no universal role, and even within a single role what might be a good job at one time may not be at another as business priorities shift. However, that does not mean it is not possible to make some general and useful comments about what counts as good. Generically, there are five elements to performing a good job as a manager:

1. Team performance.
2. Making improvements.
3. Developing the team.
4. Making a personal contribution.
5. Being a good corporate citizen.

Doing a good job is a result of fulfilling the tasks well, but it is also about choosing the right things to do. Your attention should be towards your team and its task at hand, whilst regularly scanning across the wider organisation to see where else you can add value. However you decide to focus your attention, do not confuse doing a good job with excelling in your career. They are related but are not the same (see the fourth section).

Team performance

It is not your performance, and it is not the performance of any individual or sub-group, that counts. It is the overall performance of the team that matters (see pp. 82–94 and 109–23). Of course, you will have higher and lower performers, but your fundamental goal must be to ensure the team completes the necessary work.

One lesson successful managers learn is to manage expectations. What 'the necessary work' is, is not fixed. Your forecasts and what you repeatedly say will shape the understanding of what is 'the necessary work'. That is not to say you will never be faced with demanding and even unreasonable requests, but that you have an opportunity to influence this.

A manager who says yes to everything, or who never advises what is and is not possible, will face constantly increasing workloads and will never be judged to be doing a good job.

Making improvements

As you manage your team you will find areas where there are issues, and where improvements can be made. Many improvements can be made as part of the daily routine of work. Each improvement may be tiny, but over time the cumulative effect on productivity can be huge. Your aim is to maximise the long-term productivity of the team.

You should encourage your team members to identify ways to improve their work, and empower them to make small changes as they go along. With any changes there is a risk of unforeseen disruption, so you need to set some guidelines about how much change team members can make without coming to you for authorisation.

However, not everything can be improved as part of everyday work. Some improvements need investment. Such improvements will always require some of your team's time, and may require budget. In this situation you have to make a trade-off between the short-term losses in productivity whilst team members work on improvements and the longer-term increase in productivity (see pp. 158–64).

Developing the team

More than anything else, what will differentiate you as a really good manager from the average, is how you help the individuals in the team to develop. There are many factors which will contribute towards your development of staff. Some of the most important are:

- Your behaviour as a role model for the rest of the team.
- The style of management you adopt and the coaching you give (see pp. 95–100).

- The risks you take in terms of the work you allocate individuals (see pp. 173–9).

- The opportunities you create for team members, from training courses to working on projects outside of the team.

There are two aspects to helping people develop. The first is helping individuals to develop the skills and capabilities to be of more value to business. The second is helping individuals for their own career benefit. Your priority as a manager is the former. Where possible, you should also do the latter as it creates goodwill, deepens relationships and often is in the interest of the business anyway.

Making a personal contribution

You are not just a manager, you are a member of the business as well. You are part of your own manager's team. One aspect of doing a good job is the tasks you personally pick up and work on. Most often these are activities your boss asks you personally to do (see pp. 55–61), but they may also be as a member of a cross-functional task force or project team.

Let me give you some examples. Your boss may ask you to do some research on new technology and write a presentation for an upcoming management meeting. You choose to coach a less experienced peer who is struggling with his team. You could be involved in sorting out some problems in a different area of the business from the one your team works in.

If you have any choice, select the activities you are involved in with care, as you can easily get swamped and have no time left to be a manager. But from time to time do pick up personal tasks.

Your boss depends on you and her judgement affects your career progression. Having a helpful attitude to her is beneficial. More generally, being involved in important projects provides a great chance to get visibility. It can expose useful information, increase your influence, develop your own skills and help in your career progression.

Being a good corporate citizen

You are not an isolated team, but a part of the overall organisation. In business there will always be tasks that are missed, problems that arise, and help that is needed that fall outside of your or seemingly anyone else's remit. The good corporate citizen is the employee who is always ready to step in when such problems arise.

The willingness to jump and give you or your team's support to activities that fall outside of your understood remit is important. However, you should avoid being a good corporate citizen if it is at the cost of your core role, unless requested or sanctioned by your boss. Sometimes managers become so interested or fixated on solving an issue in the business that they lose track of the day job. This is to be avoided.

Try not to do work that should be done by someone else. If you see a gap there can be a temptation for the good corporate citizen to fill it. There is a risk in filling in for someone else. Whilst in the short run it may solve problems, in the longer run it makes them worse. The individuals or team who should be doing the work do not learn and do not have any incentive for picking up the tasks. Additionally, the problem is never exposed for management attention.

Pressures to be resisted

You cannot do everything you might want to do. Your ability to do as much as possible depends on allocating the scarcest resource you have in the most efficient way possible. That resource is your time. You must make regular and conscious decisions about where you are going to allocate your time and where you will not.

In making decisions about your personal time allocation, there are several pressures to resist:

- Always completing the most urgent tasks. Some urgent tasks must be done, but if you only focus on the urgent you will never find time to do the important.

- Always responding to who shouts loudest. Sometimes the people with the loudest voices are far from the most important. Important and powerful people do not have to shout, but still must be listened to.

- Trying to do a little bit of everything. To fulfil tasks in sufficient quality you will never be able to do everything. Trying to do everything just leads to nothing being completed. You must prioritise and this means saying no to some activities.

- Trying to do everything so it is perfect. Perfectionists struggle as managers. You must make compromises – otherwise you will focus on too small a set of tasks.

Work on this more if ...

- You struggle to prioritise your own time and workload.
- You do not know where to focus and are unsure whether what you are doing is a good job.

Manager's checklist

- Make sure your team achieve their necessary level of performance, making improvements to increase long-term productivity where possible.

- Constantly seek opportunities to develop team members.

- Make a personal contribution where it adds value and helps your career.

- Selectively be a good corporate citizen, but avoid doing so if it creates further problems.

- Optimise your own performance by managing your time and resisting inappropriate pressures.

What else do you need to do?

What is this about and why is it important?

The preceding seven parts cover a wide range of management activities, but there is much else for you to do. Asking what a manager needs to do is one of those *how long is a piece of string?* sort of questions. The answer varies from manager to manager and depends on the context. However, there is much that is common between management roles. I have selected six vital activities to introduce:

- Satisfying customers and managing suppliers.
- Thinking about the future, and designing changes.
- Making improvements.
- Plans, forecasts and budgets.
- Administrative processes.
- Reporting and presentations.

There are many reasons for you to do each management activity. There are practical reasons: making your life easier, working more efficiently, or adding value to the business. There are political reasons: maintaining relationships and impressing stakeholders. Then there are the rituals of business. Business has a culture and certain expectations are built into this. As a manager in business you have to work within this culture and will find yourself doing things just because this is the way things are done. Try to understand the practical, political and ritual aspects of tasks.

The annual budgeting process is an example of a task that has practical, political and ritual aspects. Practically, you need a budget to do your job. Politically, you need the right support in place to get the budget you require, and the way you use your budget affects your relationships. Ritually, there are certain ways budget processes are expected to work, for better or worse.

When considered rationally it makes sense to cease some business rituals, or to find better ways. But unless you are senior or influential you are often better off sticking to the conventions. One of the challenges of management is deciding when it is worth taking a risk and challenging a business habit and when, sub-optimal though it is, you keep your head down and do it in the way it has always been done.

Objectives for managers

- To form a balanced picture of the range of activities a manager needs to do and the reasons for doing them.
- To develop the capabilities to perform competently all common management tasks.

Common issues in achieving these objectives

- Too narrow a perspective of what managers need to do.
- Lack of guidance to managers based on the assumption that all managers know what they should do.
- Focusing on the practical reasons for every task, and not being aware of political or ritual rationale.

The management guide

Satisfying customers and managing suppliers

The starting point for designing the work of your team should be an understanding of your customers' desires. Those customers may be internal, in the form of departments your team do work for or provide inputs to, or external in the form of customers who pay for the work of your team. If you want to understand and fulfil customer needs, it helps to have a basic understanding of marketing, but it is not essential. What is essential is entering into dialogue with your customers – to listen to them, to understand their requirements, and to set expectations as to what you can and cannot do.

To enable you to provide the products and services to your customers, you take inputs from suppliers. Again your supplier may be another department that does the preceding steps in a business process, or may be external suppliers whom you pay for inputs. Either way you will get the best from your suppliers if you learn to define your requirements clearly and develop the skills to negotiate to get the best from them.

For more ideas also read the last section of Part 4 (pp. 101–6).

Thinking about the future and designing changes

Business constantly develops, and it is best if this development is deliberate rather than accidental or ad hoc tinkering. This is where strategy comes in. The role of strategy in business is to set direction for the organisation, and to align the behaviour of the organisation towards that direction. Strategy is forward looking.

Strategy is one of the most talked about and probably overused words in management. But businesses definitely benefit from strategies. As a manager you need to understand and interpret the business strategy for your team. As discussed on pp. 82–8, you should have a vision or direction for your team, usually related to the broader business strategy.

A vision for the future becomes reality by making changes to your existing departmental inputs, outputs, organisation, processes and systems. You do not need to be an organisational, process or systems design expert. But you will find it far easier to think about how you achieve your strategy if you have an awareness of these topics, and are able to enter into practical discussions concerning them.

Making improvements

Improvements are achieved by making changes to your ways of working. Such changes can be anything from minor procedural tweaks to radical transformations which completely alter processes, tools and organisational structure.

There are various tools which help in making improvements in business. Most managers do not need to be experts in any of these tools, but an awareness of them is essential. You must have an ability to enter into discussions concerning business improvements. The sort of techniques I am thinking of include project and change management, and specialised methodologies such as Lean and Six Sigma.

Many of the big changes will be enforced on you as part of corporate change initiatives. Innovative teams don't wait for these initiatives, but are continuously improving. The most important factor in continuous improvement is the attitude of the team. Continuous improvement will thrive when you encourage, promote and reward everyday enhancements in working methods by your team.

For more ideas also read the last section of Part 6 (pp. 158–64).

Plans, forecasts and budgets

Businesses work to an annual cycle. The cycle starts with planning and forecasting for the following year. There is a seemingly logical train of activities: you plan for the following year, forecast the resources you require, and create a budget based on this forecast. Underlying this process is your ability to estimate. If you plan to do x, y and z, what headcount, money and other resources will you require?

There is a fault in these processes. In business, accurate and detailed plans and budgets tend to be favoured, but as was discussed on pp. 167–72, the future is not reliably predictable. What you will be doing at the end of the year will not accurately map back onto the plans you made at the beginning of the year (unless you are in an unusually stable business). Additionally, to be able to estimate correctly the following have to be right: your business assumptions, the baseline information you calculate from, any algorithms used to calculate budgets, and your expectations about the projects and changes you will make.

The likelihood of this all being correct is low. So, why bother? The primary reason is that you have no choice. You need a budget to operate. It's easier and more practical to make adjustments against a baseline plan than to ask for money every time you want to do anything. It is also what is expected in business.

Budgeting is as much about setting expectations and gaining approval to use resources as it is about accurately predicting the future. A good budget is not a prediction set in stone – it reflects your understanding of the risk. You want a budget which does not restrict you, but keeps your options open for changes as the year progresses.

To gain a budget you must be willing to argue convincingly for what you require. If you are being asked to give up budget, do not give it up without a fight. The budget round is not the time to play the perfect corporate citizen and hand your budget over to other teams. You will get no thanks for doing this if it means you cannot do your job.

If you do not get the necessary budget you will regret it for the rest of the year and sometimes longer. Often next year's budget will be this year's plus or minus a few per cent. When you get a new team, argue for all the budget you need, else you may always struggle. This is not about being greedy, but about making your job achievable taking account for risk.

For more ideas also read the first section of Part 7 (pp. 167–72).

Administrative processes

Once an organisation gets beyond a certain size it will develop a series of administrative processes. Such processes cover topics such as finance, payroll, various HR-related activities, getting IT equipment allocated or fixed, holiday booking, logistics for booking meeting rooms and so forth. Most administrative processes start out as important value-adding tasks, but unless they are monitored properly have a habit of becoming bureaucratic.

In most cases administrative processes are all nominally mandatory, but you will find they are a significant burden and if you do all of them to their fullest extent you will run out of time for other activities. Therefore you need to develop an understanding of what is *really* mandatory and to what level of quality it needs to be done. Then do what is really mandatory, but also what else you think adds value or is required to manage your risk.

Another aspect of administrative processes is ensuring compliance to them. For example, you may have to ensure that your staff maintain health and safety records. Here lies a challenge for managers. Every administrative process you do takes valuable time and every one you ignore adds risk.

Should you incorrectly judge a process not to be essential when your boss thinks it is, you may find yourself in trouble. Additionally, some of these processes are only truly important when something goes wrong. A good example is health and safety tracking. In a normal situation, it can seem like an unnecessary burden, but if something goes wrong, not having the correct health and safety records can convert a straightforward situation into a difficult one.

What can you do? You should observe what other managers in your business do and adopt what is helpful. But do not fall into the trap of simply doing everything others do. Do not cut corners with administrative processes unless you are comfortable doing it. When something goes wrong it may well be you personally who is held to account.

Reporting and presentations

An aspect of all management roles is reporting and making presentations. There is much more to understand about these topics than can be covered in a few lines.

All managers are both consumers and producers of information. Much of this production and consumption happens informally, but important contributions are formal reports and presentations. They are essential for collecting and disseminating information and ideas around organisations. As such, it is critical for you to understand what reports and presentations you should read or attend, and what you should be contributing to. A significant element of your time will be spent doing this – it is therefore important to critically assess where your reporting and presenting priorities lie.

But reports and presentations should not only be thought of as concerned with information dissemination. They are part of the ritual of management. The way you present, the frequency of presentation, the audiences you present to and the impression you give when you present are important influences on career progression. Being perceived as a source of valuable information, a good presenter and someone who attracts influential audiences will help to drive your career.

Work on this more if ...

- You are unaware of all the parts of a manager's role.
- You do not know how to prioritise between different aspects of your role.

Manager's checklist

- There is a wide range of tasks for managers to perform, done for practical, political and ritual reasons.

- You should understand your place in the value chain – knowing your customers' needs and getting what you require from your suppliers.

- Strategy and change are associated with a range of techniques. You usually do not need to be an expert in these techniques but you should be sufficiently aware to be able to contribute to management discussions.

- Forecasting and budgeting is a flawed but vital process. Make sure you get the budget you require, or you may regret it for years to come.

■ You may have to cut corners on administrative processes, but think about the risk you are taking before you do.

■ Reporting and presentation help in the sharing of information, and also influence career progression.

Rights, wrongs, ethics and behaviour

What is this about and why is it important?

For a long time the impact of business on individuals, society and culture has been a matter of concern and debate. Criticism of the profit motive stretches back to antiquity. More recently an interest in *business ethics* has developed. The level of interest waxes and wanes, but every time business is seen as contributing to major problems, such as the recent world recession, business ethics moves back up the agenda. In most companies ethics as well as commercialism influences decisions and actions.

One visible example of the impact of business ethics is CSR (Corporate Social Responsibility). CSR is a bundle of policies, procedures and attitudes in a company. CSR is intended to be a self-regulating mechanism to ensure a business's active compliance with laws, regulations, ethical standards and other established norms of behaviour. The effectiveness and appropriateness of CSR is still subject to significant debate. A certain level of cynicism is also associated with CSR. Some commentators see it as a smokescreen, used to pretend a business is being ethical when in practice nothing has changed.

Most companies strive to comply with all applicable laws and regulations. Legal and regulatory compliance are not trivial issues, but ethics goes beyond such compliance. It is not difficult to imagine many scenarios which are legal, but which are unethical. A simple, practical way to think of ethics is as the beliefs which enable you to decide how to do good, and equally important, how to avoid doing harm. This simple and practical way can soon lead you into controversial areas and complex debates. My aims in this section are comparatively modest. I want to raise the issue of ethics as part of your management approach.

Objectives for managers

■ To be conscious of your own and your business's ethical position and to undertake management actions and decisions which are compliant with it.

■ To be able to deal with ethical dilemmas.

Common issues in achieving these objectives

■ Lack of sufficiently thorough consideration of ethics on a day-to-day basis.

■ Lack of clarity over who are relevant stakeholders.

■ Complexity of, and lack of transparency in, stakeholder interests.

The management guide

Ethics is a personal issue. Although many of your ethical beliefs will be common to the society and culture you have been brought up in, your ethical beliefs will be your own. Within a business there will be people with a range of ethical beliefs, some complementary and some conflicting with yours.

What role does ethics play in management? There are lots of situations in which you will make decisions and exhibit behaviours which have an ethical component. Ethics touches onto issues of fairness, keeping promises, respecting the rights of your team members and obligations towards them, and generally considering the interests of others. You will be judged as ethical or unethical depending on your behaviour. As the manager you will, to some extent, set the ethical context for your team.

In any ethical decision you must be sensitive to the norms of the organisation you are working for, and the wider social culture in which it exists. If your employer has a CSR policy then you should be aware of it. What may be more difficult is understanding the relationship between the documented CSR position and the expected practical effect it has on everyday work. This can only be determined through experience. Whatever the ethical position of your employer, you must resist the temptation to outsource your ethical decisions to the overall business culture, just following how everyone else behaves. We each have a responsibility to consider ethics and make ethical decisions we feel are right.

Ethics tends to be thought of in terms of unwavering absolute rules, in the form of 'thou shalt not steal'. But there is a continuous gradual evolution in ethical beliefs. For instance, some forms of stereotyping which would have been regarded as acceptable one or two generations ago are now regarded as ethically as well as legally unacceptable.

Constraint or guiding principle?

Some activities have an ethical dimension but many do not. Taking a trivial example, when you kick a football there is no ethical dimension to it. Making the example more relevant, some professions are intimately tied with ethics: think of medicine or working in a charity. But business is neither inherently immoral nor moral. Business can be pursued in an immoral fashion, and a business can be pursued to achieve moral outcomes.

What the ethical responsibilities of businesses are is a contentious issue.

One view is that business does not exist to promote ethics. To the proponents of this view, ethics is important, but acts as a constraint upon business. This type of thinking is typified in the form of: *we can do what we want as long as it is not unethical, so we should not do x because it is unethical.* This is a common perspective for managers in business. Most people would agree that businesses and management should not pursue activities which are clearly unethical.

Another view is that business has a positive responsibility to promote ethics. This type of thinking is typified in the form of: *we should do y because it is the most ethically beneficial.* To proponents of this view, ethics is one of the central considerations in all decisions. Historically, this view has not been widespread in business. It is still a controversial view, but support is growing, for example in those businesses that emphasise CSR.

Avoiding unethical decisions is reasonably clear cut. Having a positive responsibility to take the most ethical path is much more challenging for managers. Making decisions and following a path of activity because it is the optimal ethical approach is complex and regularly raises dilemmas.

Stakeholders and interests

The concept of ethics is closely linked to the notion of interests. Making an ethical decision requires you to determine whose interests you should consider, and whose interests are primary. A common word in business is *stakeholder*. A stakeholder is simply an individual or group with an interest that you should consider.

A business is an organisation that has a range of overlapping interests. For simplicity, as a manager you can consider five groups of stakeholders whose interests you need to consider:

- Yourself.
- Your team members.
- The interests of other members of the business.
- The interests of your customers.
- Other interests (society, environment etc.).

There is some controversy as to how far your ethical considerations have to stretch and the nature of those ethical responsibilities. So for example, you may consider you have a responsibility to consider the ethical implications of any decision for your team, but not for society as a whole. Generally, it is not possible to paint a black and white boundary line at which your ethical responsibility ends. Each situation is unique, and whose interests should be considered depends on that situation.

Dealing with ethical dilemmas

There is a certain level of challenge in determining whether a course of action is right or wrong, but the real challenge of ethics is dealing with ethical dilemmas. Ethical dilemmas occur when the alternative options all have positive and negative ethical implications – and you must assess which is the optimal. Often there is no right choice, just a least bad option.

The source of many ethical dilemmas is a conflict of interests between different stakeholders. The starting point for good ethical decision making must be for you to have a perspective on who are the relevant stakeholders and what are their interests.

For example, dilemmas arise:

■ Where you are being encouraged to pursue a path of activity for business reasons which is contrary to your ethical beliefs: for instance, being asked to terminate a supplier, as a cheaper alternative has been found, when you have encouraged the supplier to invest heavily to support your business, implying there would be long-term opportunity for them.

■ Where the interests of the business and your team clash: for example, being asked to promote the loyalty of team members to the business whilst being aware that you may need to make redundancies in future.

■ Where the optimal decision for a business would not be the optimal outcome for a group of external stakeholders: for instance, being asked to offshore a team when you know that it will create employment issues in the location the team is being offshored from.

There are no universally optimal answers to situations like these. Ethics should not be a trivial concern for managers, but neither should ethics regularly result in intensely complex analysis. Occasionally in your career you may face really deep ethical challenges, but they will be rare. Most of the time common sense, pragmatism and reasoned judgement will enable you to make good ethical decisions.

Work on this more if ...

- You do not consciously consider ethics in terms of your decisions or behaviours, but just follow the norms of the business.
- You regularly face ethical dilemmas which you struggle with.
- Your business is moving from a position of avoiding the unethical to positively promoting the ethical.

Manager's checklist

- Ethical considerations should be an important part of your management decision making and behaviour.
- Ethics can be understood as a constraint limiting action, or as a positive set of guidance for action. Business tends to perceive it as a constraint, but increasingly it is being used as positive guidance.
- Most ethical issues arise from the conflicting interests of different stakeholders.

Excelling in your career

What is this about and why is it important?

There is a standard type of question used in recruitment interviews. It takes a form like *where do you see yourself in five years' time?* or *what do you want to achieve in your career?* I am dubious of the value of this question, but I understand its aim: to explore your career vision and your drive to excel.

There are two related aspects of excelling in a management career:

1. Improving as a manager.
2. Achieving career progress and promotions.

Simply by working as a manager you will improve your management skills over time. As you improve, you may find that your career progresses and you are periodically promoted. You can approach improvement and progression as the chance outcome of your work. Alternatively, you can deliberately seek to improve and progress, which is much more effective.

This section provides tips on managing your career to be successful.

Objectives for managers

- To continuously develop your skills to become a great manager.
- To maximise your opportunities to progress in your career.

Common issues in achieving these objectives

- Not understanding how to improve or progress.
- Unwillingness to adapt behaviour.
- Confusing doing a good job with reasons for promotion.

The management guide

Improving as a manager

You can learn a lot about management by reading books, attending courses, or discussing it with practitioners. But you cannot be taught to be a manager. You have to learn through experience. Management requires dealing with people and making judgements. These are experience-based skills.

We looked in the first section of this part at *what* being a good manager entails. Improving requires experience and a clear understanding of what being good means. The list below gives key tips in *how* to become a better manager.

- *Be self-reflective*: review what you find is effective and what is not so effective. It is easy to observe failings in others; it is harder to notice them in ourselves. One of the most powerful drivers for improvement is honest self-reflection.

- *Observe*: watch what other managers do. Assess what makes some managers effective and what makes others ineffective. There is no shame in copying effective behaviour.

- *Listen*: to improve you need to be willing to hear others' opinions. Seek regular feedback and other people's views of your strengths and weaknesses. Make use of any tools available in your organisation, such as 360-degree feedback processes. Avoid discounting what you do not like to hear, but also critically assess others' feedback before accepting it at face value.

- *Select modifications to make to your behaviour*: consolidate your reflections, observations, feedback and lessons from other sources such as books. Then decide what you are going to modify. Don't think you will not benefit from changing, but also don't try and change everything at once. Focus on a few things that will make a difference to your performance. Don't worry about being imperfect – everyone is. Successful management is about improving a little at a time, not being immediately ideal.

■ *Experiment and change your management approach*: practise the modifications you have selected. When you make a change treat it as an experiment. Some changes will work, others won't. When they work and become natural to you, focus on the next one or two things you can do better.

■ *Take on risky and demanding activities*: expose yourself to challenges. You do not have to constantly take risks, but you need to take some. Choose carefully. You learn most when you are under pressure. If you want an easy life, that is fine, stick with it. But do not expect you will learn or progress that much. An undemanding and consistent job may be attractive, but it is not a learning environment.

■ *Remain willing to adapt*: understand the context you are in at any time, and adapt your behaviour relative to the situation. Be prepared to stop doing things that were successful in the past if the conditions change. The phrase 'keep reinventing yourself' is a cliché, but it is a useful one. The business environment moves on quickly and you must adapt with it.

■ *Use your time wisely*: time is your most important commodity and do not waste it. Spend it on the activities that bring value to your business, that you learn from, and that present opportunities for progress (if you want it). Think of your success in terms of the outcomes you achieve in your time, not how busy you are.

■ *Manage your ego*: when it comes to learning, your ego is your enemy. Ego makes you proud and less likely to be willing to listen or accept painful feedback. It also makes you less inclined to experiment and worry too much about the risk of making a fool of yourself.

Career progress and promotion

Progression can seem increasingly hard. You may feel that you are squeezed between long-term employees who won't retire, and new team members with talent and aspiration. Retirement is getting later and later. Every year a new set of graduates enter the employment market, all with slightly newer skills. On top of this, there can be constant pressures for cost efficiency and downsizing, meaning you risk being pushed out.

No matter how senior you are, solid management skills that you keep improving will help you go further. To be successful you should strive to do a good job, but it is not enough on its own. Promotion is not a reward for good performance. Your pay cheque and other contractual commitments are your reward. Promotion comes because there is a need for a more senior manager and you are perceived as best placed to fill it.

People who are really successful manage their career to be successful. This list below gives key tips on how you can go about this:

- **Be seen to do a good job**: from a career progression viewpoint there is no point doing a good job unless it is recognised that you have done a good job. The more powerful and influential people are aware of your work, the better.

- **Add value beyond your role**: you have a busy job, but sometimes go a little further and do things which help the business beyond the context of your day job. Businesses love the manager who gives more – as long as it is not at the cost of the day job.

- **Stay central**: making sure that the job you do is linked to the core aspects of the business. You can strive away doing a great job in the periphery of the business, but unless it is seen as central you may not be rewarded that much.

- **Work to the next level**: to be promoted you are (or should be) being judged on your capability to do work at the next level. Be judged positively by being seen to behave as a more senior manager already.

- **Observe those who are promoted**: don't bemoan the fact that you see colleagues who are less intelligent or less talented than you doing better. Work out what they are doing that helps them progress. Occasionally, it will be that they are scratching the right backs. But mostly it is because they are being seen to achieve things which you are not.

■ *Set expectations*: make clear that you expect to be promoted. A business may be perfectly happy with you in your current role. If you don't ask you may never get.

■ *Satisfy multiple stakeholders*: you cannot satisfy everyone, but unless you have a very powerful sponsor, satisfying one person only is not enough. Build the right relationships and gain supporters.

■ *Focus on your strengths*: accept the strengths you have and build on them, rather than try to be good at everything. There are certain things you must be able to do to be promoted, and if you can't you must develop them. Strive to improve the weaknesses which are holding you back, but no one is good at everything. Excel where you are really great rather than exerting huge effort becoming moderately good at things you naturally are weak at.

■ *Balance generalist and specialist skills*: your career requires broad skills. The most senior managers have a wide range of skills. But your value at any time is based on one or more specialisms. You get the highest rewards for having management skills that are rare and in-demand specialisations. However, in the longer run breadth is more important than specific skills.

■ *Coach one or more successors*: avoid being seen as indispensable in your current role. If you are indispensable it may be too risky for the business to promote you. Remove this risk by having an obvious successor in the team already trained to take over from you.

■ *Be patient for promotion, but don't wait forever*: don't get impatient and jump to new jobs every time you do not progress as you expect. There must be a more senior role available for you to be promoted into. But if such vacancies never arise or are never offered to you, sooner or later it is time to move elsewhere where your skills will be appreciated. If you do not get promoted ask your manager why. If your manager cannot define why you did not get the last promotion or what you must do in future to get one, it is time to move on.

■ *Choose the roles you take with care*: do not take every role offered to you. Only take ones that help you achieve your goals, even if it is indirectly. Additionally, you will do best in roles that suit your skills and personality. This is a challenge with your first job when you do not know what management is all about. So take a job that seems reasonable and learn. Accept that it may not be ideal. Then strive from the second job onwards to do something that gives you what you want.

Work on this more if ...

■ You have a fixed set of management skills.

■ Your career is not progressing as expected.

■ Your learning happens on an ad-hoc basis.

Manager's checklist

■ To improve self-reflect, observe and listen to feedback. Then assess this information and make modifications to your behaviour.

■ A good job will not help you to progress unless it is seen to be a good job.

■ The most successful people manage their career to be successful.

nine

The developing manager

This is the last part of the book. The preceding parts describe approaches to becoming a better manager, with each section focusing on a specific area of management. This part steps back from specifics and looks more generally at how you can most effectively approach your personal development as a manager.

Learning to be a manager never stops. It is always possible to develop more.

The chapter starts with an exploration of how you can go about getting help within your business. There is more help available than you may realise, as long as you know how to access it.

But help is not only available from inside the organisation. The second section describes other sources of help and advice obtainable independent of the organisation you are currently employed by.

The third section looks at the tools that are available to

managers, and how you should approach them. There are many powerful management tools, but they are only worth learning about if you are going to use them.

Finally, there is a discussion of your personal performance review, building on the previous discussions in the first and last sections of Part 8. This is not just a business ritual you must go through; it as an important mechanism for shaping your career and your progress.

Help is at hand

What is this about and why is it important?

Successful people are often presented as self-sufficient. Self-sufficiency is a useful aptitude in many situations. As a manager in business you are expected to have a high degree of self-reliance, by forming an ability to work independently and autonomously. But the whole point of a business organisation is to consolidate resources within a single entity to work together to achieve common objectives. Help is not only available – it is an essential feature of business that people help each other constructively. If not, why bother to be in the same organisation?

Yet there is a significant difference in the ability of different managers to find and use the help that is required. Becoming a successful manager is partially about your individual skills and abilities, but these will only take you so far. Success is also about locating and applying the knowledge and resources of the organisation to support your goals.

Help can be verbal: comments, suggestions, recommendations, instructions, tips and ideas. It can come with the provision of resources you would not otherwise have. Help is important to your team. One of the aspects of your role is creating the environment in which your team thrives. Your team is more likely to thrive if you encourage a culture in which team members help each other, and you also ensure team members have access to the resources they need to do their job.

Objectives for managers

- To gain access to the resources you and your team need to achieve your objectives.
- To develop a working environment for your team where team members constructively help each other.

Common issues in achieving these objectives

- Lack of clarity about what resources are available.
- Imprecise understanding of team member needs for help.
- Unwillingness to search out sources of assistance.
- Other managers' or teams' unwillingness to support you or your team.

The management guide

In most businesses there are many people who are able to help you. There are your team members, some of whom will know things you do not. There is your boss, who will have useful experience in areas you do not. There are your peers, some of whom will have ideas and approaches which could be helpful to you. On top of this, businesses have specialists you can go to for help such as HR, IT and finance.

No matter how tight the budgets are there is normally some additional money tucked away in one or other senior manager's departmental or divisional budgets, if only you know how to access it. There may be people who are not 100% busy and have time to help your team. There will be a wide range of resources available, from training courses to meeting rooms and other facilities.

The list of resources available in a large business goes on and on. The starting point for being able to access these resources is to understand what resources are available, or to have a reliable network of contacts who can point you in the right direction when you need help.

Resourceful managers

Resourceful managers have a variety of characteristics. Generally, they have a large network of contacts. In fact, one of the primary reasons to develop a network is to be able to get the help you want, when you want it. Resourceful managers tend to be creative when it comes to thinking about sources of help. They have a positive attitude to asking for help, and are resilient, not being put off the first time someone says no to a request for help. Resourceful managers are good negotiators, able to understand objections to providing help and give effective counter-arguments.

The most successfully resourceful managers are also well liked. This makes people more willing to listen to their requests and help them out when they ask.

Why will help be offered?

One of the best starting points for getting the help and resources you need is to consider why someone would help you. In a business, the most obvious answer is that it is their job to help you. This is true in some situations, but thinking this way will only get you so far. Much of the most useful knowledge and resources is not yours by right, and there may be contention for these resources between you and other managers and teams.

People will help you if they think it is worthwhile. This is partially about you explaining the value to the business of helping you out, but also on a more personal level, making sure that the potential helper thinks he is likely to get support back when he needs it. People help others who are helpful. Help is best sought when it's seen to be reciprocal. To get help you should try to be a source of assistance yourself. This requires openness and a willingness on your behalf to be helpful, and also that you have some knowledge or resource that others perceive as useful to them.

You will also find it far easier to get the help you require if people like you. It sounds trite, but it is true that people are more willing to give time and support to those individuals they like. Developing friendly relationships at work is as much about having productive relationships as about making the working environment pleasant.

Asking for help

To access help you need to ask for it, and there are more or less effective ways of asking. Often in asking for help you need to be confident and assertive. But this does not mean you should be unpleasant. Whenever you ask for help, consider that you may need to ask for it again, and the simple guidance of asking politely is often worth sticking with. However, you must judge the situation and the personalities you are dealing with. It is true that *he who shouts loudest* should not and does not always win arguments for resources, but sometimes having the loudest voice does work.

Ideally, requests for help are timely, by which I mean you give the helper sufficient notice to be able to help you without disrupting their own work. Unfortunately, in many situations your need for assistance is urgent. Therefore as you develop your network try to set the expectation that you may ask for help in future, and where possible, you will return the favour.

When you ask for help be precise about the support you need. It is frustrating for the helper and unproductive to be unclear or ambiguous in your requests for assistance.

The helpful team culture

The final point about help is to create the environment in which team members support each other. You can achieve this by role-modelling the behaviour you want. Regularly offer help to your team members. Praise and reward those members of the team who help each other, those who are resourceful, and those who develop skills which are valuable and useful to others. But this must always be balanced by reminding people that whilst it is good to be helpful, this should not be at the cost of not completing any high-priority and important aspects of their own work.

Work on this more if ...

- You do not have access to the resources or information to complete your work.

■ You struggle to get support and assistance from other members of the organisation.

Manager's checklist

■ There is normally a wide variety of resources available in your business to support your work – provided you know about them and how to access them.

■ The basis for getting assistance as and when you need it, is a good network of relationships.

■ Before asking for help, consider why the helper will help or may resist. Develop arguments or approaches which build on their desire to help you or overcome their resistance.

■ When asking for help be timely and precise about your need.

■ Develop a culture in which team members support each other.

Reaching externally

What is this about and why is it important?

Management has been thought, spoken and written about for a long time. It is not only an employment discipline, it is a market with a wide range of products and services targeted at managers, this book being an example of a product created for managers. By reaching beyond your organisation, you will find a rich source of information, advice, tools and support.

In choosing external resources, be selective in what you listen to and invest time or money in. Some of the products and services are fantastic and are free or at least good value for money. Others are expensive and will have minimal impact on your skills or your progress.

It is often worth seeking out the less common sources of ideas. If you learn what everybody else does, you will develop the same skills. If you want to differentiate yourself from others, you need to develop some unique skills.

Management is subject to fads, which should be watched out for. Some fashions come and disappear quickly. Others become the new thinking of the future. If you don't keep track of the ideas and terminology of the lasting trends in management you can appear outdated. A few fads are profound. Many are simply new ways of labelling old ideas.

Topics like total quality management and business process re-engineering were once fads. Few managers now spend much time talking about quality circles. But if you picked up on them when they first arose you would have been in demand. Today, the ideas of embedding quality into work, and organising businesses around customer-focused processes are basic concepts that are taken for granted.

Some managers are reluctant to invest in external resources, feeling that it is their employer's role to train them or that they spend enough time at work or thinking about work. These are valid points. Your employer should invest in your development and you should have a good work–life balance. But it is your career. The only person whom it really matters to is you. There may be skills you want to develop that your employer is not interested in. Also, it is a competitive world. You may not want to invest any more time in your professional development, but if your peers do and you don't, you may be at a disadvantage.

Objectives for managers

- To find a wide range of external support to help you fulfil your role and make progress in your career.
- To keep up to date with useful new ideas in management.

Common issues in achieving these objectives

- Awareness of the range of products and services available.
- Readiness to invest time or money in external resources.
- Time to research and locate appropriate external resources fully.

The management guide

External coaches, mentors and advisers

One of the most obvious, and often most powerful, ways of finding help and assistance in your career is to have one or more coaches, mentors or other advisers. Such individuals do not have to be part of your organisation. If you read a biography of any successful business person it is likely you will find them mentioning someone who has been critical to their success. Often this person has remained a supporter as the individual has changed roles and employers.

If you are a senior manager, your organisation may invest in a coach for you. If you have the opportunity I would try it. However, I would be quite selective about whom I chose as my coach. Whilst the skills and approaches of coaches at one level seem fairly consistent, in practice the capabilities of coaches vary hugely and you need somebody comfortable to work with.

Personally investing in a professional coach can be worthwhile, but it is not a low-cost option. However, there are many people who are happy to provide mentoring or subject-specific advice to you. Often the simplest way to get this help is just to ask them.

Courses and accreditation

There are thousands of different accreditations and qualifications, especially once you consider sector- and role-specific types of accreditation. In some roles (financial adviser, accountant etc.) a level of accreditation is mandatory, but for managers, generally, this is not so.

If you are interested in business and a management career, then starting with some form of business degree can be helpful. However, the qualification of choice is the MBA.

There are three reasons to do an MBA:

- to develop a useful toolkit to help you perform your management role;
- to develop a network of professional contacts;
- as a badge that differentiates you from other potential employees.

If are thinking about doing an MBA, go into the process with your eyes open. It can be expensive, time consuming and hard work. It can be very helpful, but many managers do an MBA expecting it to change their career dramatically, only to be disappointed.

The quality and the credibility of the courses vary hugely. An MBA from a top school will always be valuable (although at present some are devalued because of the association of the schools with key business leaders who were perceived as central to causing the recent economic crisis). The credibility of some of the less well-known schools is low. By doing an MBA with one of

these institutions you may well learn useful skills, but the qualification alone will not open many doors.

Societies and associations

There are a range of societies and associations for managers.
The most well known in the UK is the Chartered Management
Institute (I am a member of an affiliated body). These organisations offer information, networks, events and various kinds of
support and levels of membership and accreditation.

We are moving to an era of greater accreditation in which
membership of a professional society is seen as more and more
important. But management is still a long way from professions
like engineering or veterinary practice where membership of
the relevant body is essential to practice. Joining a management
organisation is largely a personal choice and you need to decide
on whether you like this sort of thing and will get value from it.
Professional recognition may marginally differentiate you from
other candidates when applying for a role, but it will rarely be a
significant factor in your ability to gain it.

Online resources

There are thousands and thousands of web sites with information,
opinions and resources for managers. It is a volatile landscape,
and new sites are cropping up all the time. I contribute to a few.

Examples of sites which have some useful content are:

1. www.businessballs.com
2. www.thinkingmanagers.com
3. www.management-issues.com
4. www.management.about.com
5. www.themanager.org
6. www.managementhelp.org

Many business thinkers maintain blogs, and these can be a great
way of keeping yourself abreast of current thinking for a fairly

small investment of time at any one period. Most of the major consultancy and business services organisations also have strong online presences, many of which contain articles and papers.

Journals

Magazines and journals, online or print versions, are useful ways to keep in touch with current management thinking, and for book reviews. There are hundreds of journals, but I have picked three as examples of useful reference sources:

1. *Management Today*;
2. *Harvard Business Review*;
3. *International Journal of Management*.

The first is an example of an excellent regular periodical with a range of business articles, opinions and news. The second is probably the most well-known business journal in the world. Many influential management trends started and are analysed in this journal. The third is an academic journal, which may not appeal to everyone, but if you are a fan of the academic papers then it is a good source.

Books

You cannot learn management from books alone, but they can give you helpful direction and speed you on your way to being a well-rounded and experienced manager. A choice of books is personal, depending on the style of writing you like.

Rather than list hundreds of management books I have chosen the ones that I think are particularly useful or insightful and relevant to the contents of this book. Not all of these books were written as management books, but they are all helpful, even if that help is as simple as cutting through management hubris.

1. Marcus Aurelius, *Meditations* (the quotes in Part 7 are from the Penguin edition, 2004, translated by Maxwell Staniforth)
2. Chris Blake, *The Art of Decisions: How to Manage in an Uncertain World* (Financial Times Prentice Hall, 2008)

3. Eliyahu M. Goldratt, *What Is This Thing Called Theory of Constraints and How Should It Be Implemented?* (North River Press, 1990)

4. Daniel Goleman, *Emotional Intelligence: Why it Can Matter More Than IQ* (Bantam Books, 2006)

5. Owen Hargie (editor), *The Handbook of Communication Skills* (Routledge, 2006)

6. Ros Jay, *How to Manage Your Boss: Developing the Perfect Working Relationship* (Prentice Hall Business, 2002)

7. Linda A. Hill, *Becoming a Manager: How New Managers Master the Challenges of Leadership* (Harvard Business School Press, 2003)

8. Henry Mintzberg, *Managing* (Financial Times Prentice Hall, 2009)

9. Richard Newton, *Financial Times Briefings: Change Management* (Financial Times Prentice Hall, 2011)

10. Jo Owen, *The Death of Modern Management: How to Lead in the New World Disorder* (John Wiley, 2009)

11. Peter S. Pande and Larry Holpp, *What Is Six Sigma?* (McGraw-Hill, 2002)

12. Steven D'Souza, *Brilliant Networking: What the Best Networkers Know, Say and Do* (Prentice Hall, 2011)

13. Robert C. Solomon, *Business Ethics* (in *A Companion to Ethics*, edited by Peter Singer; Blackwell, 1993)

14. Nassim Nicholas Taleb, *Fooled by Randomness* (Penguin, 2007)

15. Paul R. Timm, *How to Hold Successful Meetings: 30 Action Tips for Managing Effective Meetings* (Career Press, 1997)

16. Marcel van Assen, Gerben van den Berg and Paul Pietersma, *Key Management Models: The 60+ models every manager needs to know* (Financial Times Prentice Hall, 2009)

17. John Whitmore, *Coaching for Performance: GROWing Human Potential and Purpose – the Principles and Practice of Coaching and Leadership* (Nicholas Brealey, 2009)

Work on this more if ...

■ You feel you need help, but are not satisfied with that on offer within your organisation and do not know where else to seek it from.

Manager's checklist

■ There is a wide range of products and services targeted at managers, including management coaches, training courses and qualifications, societies and associations, online resources, journals and books.

■ To extend your professional development beyond that offered by your employer or to differentiate yourself from your peers, explore and utilise these products and services.

■ Be critical about your selection. Some are helpful, but others are expensive and will have little impact on your career.

■ Watch out for fads in management thinking. They can be the essential trends for the future or fashions which come and go quickly without lasting impact.

The tools for the job

What is this about and why is it important?

There is a wide set of tools available to managers to help you perform your role effectively and efficiently. I use the word *tools* in the broadest sense. It includes items such as information, training courses, governance processes and reports, as well as methodologies and management models. (I could have used the word *resources*, but this tends to be specifically associated with people and money, which are excluded as they are dealt with elsewhere in this book.)

Some tools are essential for you to be able to perform your role. Other tools are optional but advisable as they will make your life far easier. Certain tools are not advisable as the effort of acquiring the tool can be greater than the benefit.

Your organisation will provide some tools directly to you, or they will come as a by-product of operational processes. However, many of the tools you need you have to acquire for yourself. Acquiring the right tools is a significant effort: for example, collecting the information to enable you to make optimal decisions can be onerous. Acquisition of tools may mean financial investment, but most often it needs your time, for instance in locating a model to help you understand and overcome a problem you are facing.

Objectives for managers

- To understand the range of tools available to managers.
- To select the best tools to invest in acquiring.
- To make optimal use of the tools available.

Common issues in achieving these objectives

- Sticking with the familiar tools.
- Belief that your situation is unique and thinking that tools from other contexts will not work in yours.
- Lack of accessible information on tools or how to acquire them.
- Unwillingness to invest time or money in acquiring the most appropriate tools.

The management guide

Expertise

Ever since the writing of Adam Smith in the 1700s, it has been understood that the central feature of efficient business is specialisation of labour based on expertise. The range and depth of expertise available to managers is huge. Professional advisers such as management consultants, accountants, lawyers, health and safety experts and so on can help you with almost any topic.

Hiring an expert every time you face a problem that requires skills you do not have is impractical. But there will be times when additional expertise is required for essential or practical reasons.

Before paying for external experts do not underestimate your own skills, those of your team members, and what else is available in your business. Often finding sufficient expertise is a matter of looking a bit deeper at what exists in the organisation. Additionally, you have the ability to research yourself. There is a huge amount of advice in books, periodicals and especially online.

However, much of this advice is what I call *know-what*. Know-what is facts, figures, information and data. Usually what you really need is *know-how*. Know-how is approaches and experiences of what works and an ability to make things happen. Know-how is far harder to gain by just reading.

Management information and measurement

Management thrives on information. Information guides decision making, measures progress and helps to direct activity. Without adequate information you work in the dark.

There are many sources of information. Some are provided to you in management reports; other information is created as part of your normal work. Most businesses have a range of systems making information accessible to you. Make full use of what information is available. However, you should not only use the information that is easily available, thinking that is all there is.

Effective management requires sufficient information. This information should be accurate, timely and frequent. Investing in improved information, if you think your decision making or understanding of the situation is inadequate, is always worthwhile. But you must be realistic. There is a cost to obtaining information and you will never have perfect information.

The types of information you collect and analyse should not be fixed. When you change ways of working you normally need to modify the information you collect and the measurements you make. What you measure and the decisions you make based on measurement will drive the behaviour and performance of your team. In the words of the old phrase – what you measure is what you get.

Models and management theories

Management has promoted the development of all sorts of theories and models to help managers make sense of their task and to perform it better. Some of these have arisen from research into management such as Porter's five forces, value chains, balanced scorecards or SWOT analysis. Others have grown up in other disciplines but can be applied to management, such as Maslow's hierarchy of needs, Belbin's Team Analysis or de Bono's Six Thinking Hats.

There are literally hundreds of models and theories (see p. 231 for a reference to a book summarising many of them). Some are powerful and useful. There is a model or theory which is applicable to most of the problems you face as a manager – with two caveats:

- Models or management theories are not laws of nature. They are useful guides to thinking. They do not provide the absolute truth in every situation.

- Most managers are aware of many theories and models, but in practice make very little reference to such tools. There is little point investing in them if you are never going to use them!

Anecdotes, intuition, heuristics and assumptions

If you have expertise, information and the right management theories or models you have the basis for the rational and effective management of your team. In reality, on a moment-by-moment basis you have to work with anecdotal information and use your intuition building on heuristics (rules of thumb), assumptions and mental models (see pp. 19–23).

This is not a weakness of your management approach, but an essential feature of it. If every time you had to make a decision, and you make hundreds every day, you gathered accurate information, and applied the appropriate management tools or algorithms, you would quickly come to a halt.

There are obvious risks in relying on anecdote and intuition. But with experience, your ability to differentiate between useful anecdotes and gossip will increase and your intuition will improve. With practice comes the ability to make better judgements based on intuition.

The problem with intuition-based mental models, heuristics and assumptions is that much is context-specific. As time passes you will find yourself moving out of familiar contexts. You need to regularly refresh and update the mental models, heuristics and assumptions you apply. Ideally, you consciously check the mental models, heuristics and assumptions so you can challenge and adapt them when required. As intuition becomes ingrained and subconscious, this becomes hard.

Management and governance processes

Once organisations and teams get beyond a certain size there has to be some form of management and governance process. By this I mean things like decision making and approval processes, reviews, regular team meetings and reports. These processes may be formalised into a documented description, but often they are informal but embedded into the behaviour or culture of the organisation.

As a manager you will be involved in the wider organisational management and governance processes, but you will also have your own management and governance process to control your team. Such processes are essential, but can easily become bureaucratic, time-consuming and non-value-adding. Structure your process to be light-touch, flexible and value-adding. Try to influence the rest of the organisation to do the same.

Power, influence and relationships

Underlying your ability to instruct, authorise or decide is the power associated with your level in the management hierarchy. In addition, you gain power from other aspects such as your expertise, or control of resources.

As was discussed on pp. 26–31, you have less power than you might expect and sometimes than you feel you need. The alternative to controlling people through power is to employ your influence. Your influencing skills depend on people's perception of you and how you exert your influence. A key aspect in your ability to influence is your relationships. Relationships will enable you to understand better what resources and tools are available to you and your team, as well as make it easier to gain access to them.

Training

A common discussion at work, especially amongst new managers, is training. You and your team members need to develop your skills. This cannot always be achieved by doing your business-as-usual work, and you will need to undertake occasional training.

Training takes many forms. There is on-the-job training, for example being exposed to different forms of work or being taken out of your normal role and allocated to an unfamiliar project. Training can also be provided through mentoring and expert advice. However, for many people the word *training* is associated with training courses in a classroom or workshop environment.

Undoubtedly training is important, but a lot of the investment in training is wasteful. Training is only of value if it results in some alteration in behaviour. If you are doing nothing differently after a training course, then you have achieved nothing of value. Such changes in behaviour are unlikely to be substantial after a single training event, and need reinforcement and the opportunity to practise.

Formal training courses provide skills, but are also a chance to build a stronger peer network. In the longer run it is often the enhancement to networks that is the greatest value from courses. Training courses are also often perceived as perks, with access to courses being provided as a reward for positive behaviour or good performance. Offering training definitely has a motivational effect for many staff.

Time

The single most valuable resource at your disposal, and the one that there will be most contention in, is your time. Managers are typically busy, and have more work to do than there is time available to complete. There are several steps that can optimise the use of your time:

- Focus on the value-adding.
- Prioritisation (see pp. 145–51).
- Minimise multitasking (see pp. 89–94).
- Delegation (see pp. 89–94).
- Design of work.

Focus on the tasks that add the most value. Everyone can get stuck doing the activities that are either urgent or enjoyable to do. Urgency should not be confused with importance, and many of those apparently urgent tasks can be ignored. How many urgent emails you answer are actually trivial and could be ignored? Your role should be enjoyable, but the most enjoyable aspects are not always the most important.

Prioritisation is extremely powerful, conceptually simple, but hard to do. However, with practice it becomes easier and easier. Many people think they are prioritising but are not prioritising effectively. A simple rule of thumb for prioritising is, after prioritising what did you stop? If the answer is nothing, you have not prioritised effectively.

Management naturally is a multitasking role, but you do not need to increase it more than necessary. Do multitask when you have to, but don't do it as a matter of choice. It is always more inefficient than working on one task at a time, when you can.

Just because a task needs to be done, does not mean you need to do it. You need to make sure important tasks are done, and are done to the level of quality required. That is normal management activity. You have a team, so delegate work to them. Team members will willingly do many of the activities you regard as part of your work.

As you become familiar with your role, you will find aspects that are inefficient. Do not live with such realities. Think about how you can design and adapt your work and the work of your team to be more effective. Making such improvements is central to the continuously improving business (see pp. 158–64).

Work on this more if ...

- You do not have the tools or resources to do your job.
- You are struggling with an aspect of your role which your peers seem to find straightforward.
- Your team members complain about the tools they have to undertake their roles.

Manager's checklist

- There is a wide range of tools and resources available to managers. Some of these are essential and others will make your life far easier. But only invest in those that are worthwhile and add value to your role.

- To optimise your performance think carefully about what tools you need and what are available and, where possible, find ways to close the gap.

Using your annual appraisal

What is this about and why is it important?

The annual appraisal is a more or less formal ceremony in most organisations. It is a ritual that has important implications. You will do annual appraisals for each of your team members, but in this section I want to focus on your appraisal with your boss.

The annual appraisal may be approached with a sense of dread and boredom for a bureaucratic process which goes through the motions but effects no real outcomes. Alternatively, there may be a feeling of excitement if rewards or promotions are in the offing. To some degree the effect of the annual appraisal is out of your control. Different organisations regard appraisals with varying levels of importance. All businesses *say* they are important, but in reality there is a spectrum from those in which appraisals are one of the critical events of the year to those in which they are a paper-based exercise justifying decisions already made. Additionally, the value depends on the seriousness and effort which your specific boss puts into the process. As was explored on pp. 62–7, many bosses are imperfect and one aspect of imperfection is treating the annual appraisal without diligence.

The annual appraisal should be an important process, and irrespective of the attitude of your organisation and your boss, you should make the best of it that you can. Making the best of your appraisal is achieved by actively managing the process rather than being a passive recipient of it.

Annual appraisals are a two-stage process, each stage of which is significant. There is a backward-looking process of reviewing your performance in the last period. This is a key determinant in any increase in rewards and career progression, and influences expectations for the year moving forward. There is also a forward-looking process in which objectives are set for the following year. This process will determine quite how demanding and achievable your task is, and will influence the opportunities you are offered in future.

Objectives for managers

- To achieve the best personal result from your annual appraisal in terms of performance review and objectives moving forward.
- To use the appraisal process to enhance your relationship with your boss.

Common issues in achieving these objectives

- Too little diligence is given to the process, it being treated as a mandatory but largely irrelevant series of steps.
- Annual appraisals being dealt with at the last minute, with too little time for sufficient data collection or for consideration and review.

The management guide

Prepare

Start by understanding the appraisal process and the associated paperwork. Each organisation has its own variant on the process, and its own behaviours and objectives that you will be assessed against. There is a certain amount of data and evidence that has to be collected to complete appraisal forms. The data is not normally complicated, but it does take time to collate. If you leave this to the end of the year what is a straightforward process can become onerous.

The process has to happen to a schedule of dates or be complete by a certain date. Often the outcome from your annual appraisal, at least as far as forward-looking objective setting, has to cascade down to the rest of your team. Their objectives cannot be set until yours are. This takes time and if you have a large team the logistics can be complicated. If you work in an open-plan office there is also the logistics of meeting-room bookings to be considered. This sounds trivial, but if everyone in the business is doing their appraisals at the same time of year, it can require some organisation to get all the meeting rooms booked that you need. Starting early helps.

For your own appraisal it is important to know what you want from the meeting and what you will need to do to get it. Outcomes to think about include:

- Justifying rewards and promotions you think are reasonable.
- Learning where you can improve and what steps you need to take to improve.
- Aligning expectations and goals between you and your boss. What do you want and need? What is realistic to expect in terms of your achievements in the following year?
- Making and justifying specific requests, for example training and development.
- Explaining and getting support for resources and help you need to do your job.
- Developing an improved mutual understanding between yourself and your boss.

It is one of the most concentrated periods of time you will have with your boss in the year, so it is a great opportunity to deepen your relationship. An appraisal should be a dialogue between you and your boss, with plenty of listening from each side.

The performance review

To achieve the best possible outcome from a performance review you need to have a positive story to tell about your performance.

Ideally, this is a story your boss is already familiar with and agrees with. A performance review is not the time for surprises; it should be a constructive and helpful dialogue. You should have a clear idea of the tone of the conversation in advance, and your boss should not be surprised by your expectations.

In preparing for a review, remember that most assessments of performance are relative, not absolute. You will be being compared to your peer group. Who are they and how have they performed? If you are ambitious you want to be seen at least as in the top quartile for performance. If you are less ambitious, you still want to be seen as in the top half. Over a long period constantly appearing in the bottom half of performance is risky in environments of regular downsizing.

Don't just think about your performance review in the few weeks running up to the appraisal. Think about it regularly throughout the year. Check that you are meeting your objectives – they can be surprisingly easy to forget when you are busy. Is what you are doing leading you to achieve the objectives and performance measures defined? If not is there anything you can do about it?

When you do a good piece of work for someone, ask them to make a note for your performance review. Having supporters with positive comments about your performance will help significantly. In contrast, if you feel you will not be able to meet objectives, manage your boss's expectations in advance.

Objective setting

Having reviewed historic progress, most annual appraisals then go on to set and agree objectives for the next year. Different organisations have different attitudes to objective setting. In some your objectives will encompass the whole of your role. In others, doing your business-as-usual role is taken for granted and the objectives are effectively 'stretch goals' to be achieved in addition to doing your daily management role.

Irrespective of your business's view of objectives, think about and negotiate them fully. The objectives you are set now will become the baseline for the performance review next year. Make sure they are worded correctly and clearly. Do not assume just because you and your boss understand each other that the wording of objectives can be lax. If your boss changes mid-year, your new boss may take the objectives literally. Additionally, if you are ever in a situation where you are being assessed for poor performance then it will be against these objectives. It is important that you believe there is some chance of achieving them.

Your boss will want you to achieve objectives that help her or him achieve their own objectives. The politician in you wants objectives which seem demanding, but which you believe are within your capabilities and resources to deliver. These need not be conflicting goals as long as you take the time and effort to understand each other. If your boss insists on very demanding objectives, ask for the resources required and the chance to achieve high rewards or promotion in return for achieving them.

As a final point, when your objectives are being set think about how achieving them will help you in your longer-term career aspirations. Few careers go in a perfectly straight line to the top, and it is normal to have some deviations as you progress. But in general terms, you want your performance objectives to be taking you in the direction you want your career to take.

Work on this more if ...

- You are not prepared for your annual appraisal.
- You are regularly surprised by what your boss says in your performance reviews.
- You have imprecise objectives, or objectives which bear minimal relationship to the role you actually perform.

Manager's checklist

- The annual appraisal process has two components: a backward-looking process which assesses your performance in the previous periods and links to rewards and promotions, and a forward-looking process which sets your objectives for next year.

■ The key to a smooth appraisal is preparation and understanding the process.

■ As the year progresses check you are meeting your objectives, and collect information and support for your end-of-year performance review.

■ Take the time to explore and negotiate your objectives fully.

Conclusion

There are large variations in what businesses do, but all businesses are built from teams and teams need managers. What is the best form of management in any one situation depends on the team members, the tasks and the context. But there are common tools and techniques of management that everyone can learn from. To help you develop, in this book we have looked at:

■ What management is, and whether it is the right career for you.

■ Understanding the needs and desires of your team.

■ Progressing through team management: starting by managing your team to perform its core role, through to developing a highly productive team.

■ Building powerful relationships around the organisation.

■ The range of things you need to do as a manager.

■ How you can advance to being a fully competent manager.

■ The sources of additional help and advice.

Good management is essential to successful organisations. We do not always take it as seriously as we should. Management is often taken for granted until it goes wrong, when it is portrayed as the root of all evils.

Perhaps this is because management is one of those activities that becomes most visible when it is done badly. Good management often goes unnoticed, with the best managers making management seem effortless. Getting to that level of management capability requires deliberate and sustained effort. Becoming a great manager takes time. But everyone is capable of becoming a great manager – if you choose to be and are willing to put the effort into developing yourself into one.

Management as a recognised discipline is hardly new, and there is a wide body of knowledge you can exploit and develop from. But in the end management cannot be learnt purely by reading books or attending courses. Management is learnt by experience. Use the advice in this book, and other sources, and apply it! It is the application of the tips, techniques, tools and ideas, and learning from the experience, that will turn you into a good manager.

I want to stress one point which has weaved its way through the whole book. There is no end point for a manager. There is no time at which you will know everything. You can always learn more. Of course, the learning curve is steepest when your career starts. If you are just starting out as a manager do not let the first few months, which many people find very challenging, put you off. It is worth the effort and it will get easier. On the other hand, if you are a very experienced manager do not let your confidence in your current capabilities stop you from learning more. Nobody is perfect, and the needs, expectations and environment of business constantly change, throwing up new challenges for managers. Dealing with these new challenges can be one of the most exciting parts of management.

Good luck with your management career. Whether you are a new manager or a well-established one, I hope your career thrives. I also hope you have found this book useful, and come back to it time and again.

Index

Read On